320.942

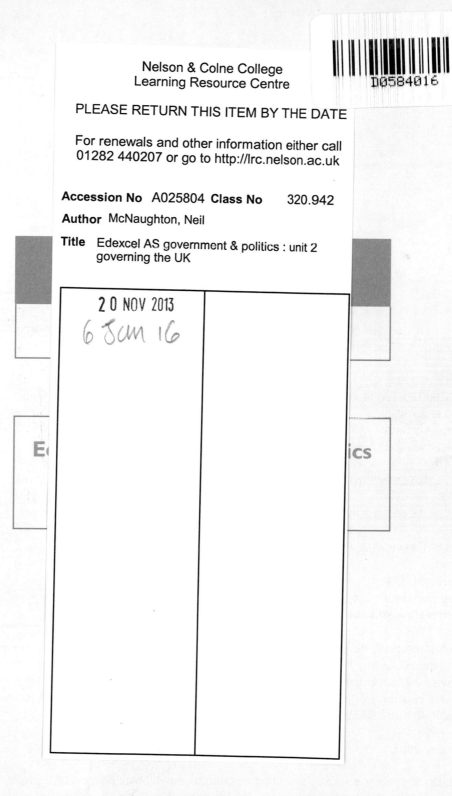

PHILIP ALLAN

Philip Allan Updates, an imprint of Hodder Education, an Hachette UK company, Market Place, Deddington, Oxfordshire OX15 0SE

Orders
Bookpoint Ltd, 130 Milton Park, Abingdon, Oxfordshire, OX14 4SB
tel: 01235 827827
fax: 01235 400401
e-mail: education@bookpoint.co.uk
Lines are open 9.00 a.m.–5.00 p.m., Monday to Saturday, with a 24-hour message answering service. You can also order through the Philip Allan Updates website: www.philipallan.co.uk

ISBN 978-1-4441-4815-2

First printed 2011
Impression number 5 4 3
Year 2015 2014 2013 2012

Printed in Dubai

Hachette UK's policy is to use papers that are natural, renewable and recyclable products and made from wood grown in sustainable forests. The logging and manufacturing processes are expected to conform to the environmental regulations of the country of origin.

Contents

Getting the most from this book

Examiner tips
Advice from the examiner on key points in the text to help you learn and recall unit content, avoid pitfalls, and polish your exam technique in order to boost your grade.

Knowledge check
Rapid-fire questions throughout the Content Guidance section to check your understanding.

Knowledge check answers
1 Turn to the back of the book for the Knowledge check answers.

Knowledge summary

Knowledge summaries
● Each core topic is rounded off by a bullet-list summary for quick-check reference of what you need to know.

Questions & Answers

Exam-style questions

Examiner comments on the questions
Tips on what you need to do to gain full marks, indicated by the icon **e**.

Sample student answers
Practise the questions, then look at the student answers that follow each set of questions.

Examiner commentary on sample student answers
Find out how many marks each answer would be awarded in the exam and then read the examiner comments (preceded by the icon **e**) following each student answer. Annotations that link back to points made in the student answers show exactly how and where marks are gained or lost.

Edexcel AS Government & Politics

About this book

This guide is for students following the Edexcel AS Government & Politics course. It aims to guide you through Unit 2: Governing the UK.

The **Content Guidance** section provides a detailed guide to the four topic areas: The constitution, Parliament, The prime minister and cabinet, and Judges and civil liberties.

The **Questions & Answers** section provides examples of examination questions with student responses at different grades, together with examiner comments.

Content guidance

About this section

This part of the book presents the key knowledge, understanding and analysis that you will need to master the topics that will enable you to answer examination questions comprehensively. You will also find regular information about key concepts. Examiner tips are provided to help you avoid mistakes and to advise you on vital information to include in particular answers.

From time to time there is a knowledge check. Here you are invited to test various key aspects of your knowledge. These checks are numbered and, at the end of the guide, you can find suggested answers. You can then see how well you did in recalling the key information.

The constitution

The role and purposes of a state constitution

Constitution A set of rules, processes and principles describing the political institutions of a state, the distribution of power among the institutions, the rights of citizens and the limits to the powers of the state.

Most state constitutions contain the following elements:
- the principles upon which the constitution is based, such as the **rule of law**
- the nature of political institutions, including their roles, powers, limitations and how their members are elected or appointed
- the relationships between institutions, the distribution of power between them and the ways in which powers are distributed between the central authority and regional and local elements of the state
- the rights and duties of citizens and the ways in which these are safeguarded
- how laws are made and enforced
- how the constitution can be amended
- the geographical components of the state
- the relationship between the state and external organisations such as the European Union (EU)

Knowledge check 1

Outline three roles of a constitution.

Features of the UK Constitution

It is uncodified and unentrenched

The UK Constitution is unusual in two main ways:

1 There are a number of different sources of the constitution, not just one source as in most countries.

2 The UK Constitution is flexible and has been able to develop and evolve naturally. Thus it is often described as an organic constitution, developing just as living organisms grow and change.

Statutes that can amend the constitution

Examples include the following:

- The Constitutional Reform Act of 2005 established a new judicial body — the Supreme Court.
- The Human Rights Act of 1998 forced all public bodies, except the UK Parliament, to abide by the European Convention on Human Rights (ECHR).
- The Scotland Act of 1998 established devolved (autonomous) government in Scotland.

Conventions that can amend the constitution

Unwritten practices, usually known as conventions, develop over time. These are unwritten rules to which everyone in the political system adheres. Thus, over the past 70 years, we have seen a number of changes as a result of new conventions. Examples include the following:

- The House of Lords should not obstruct any proposals contained in the government's most recent election manifesto (this is known as the 'Salisbury Convention' after Lord Salisbury, who first proposed it in the 1940s).
- The prime minister *must* be a member of the House of Commons and *not* the House of Lords.
- Any important constitutional changes require the approval of a referendum.

Referendums that confirm amendments to the constitution

Referendums are increasingly used to confirm constitutional change. Examples include the following:

- 1997: two referendums to decide whether power should be devolved to Scotland and Wales
- 1998: a referendum in Northern Ireland to determine whether an autonomous, power-sharing government should be established there
- 1998: a referendum to decide whether London should have its own elected mayor
- 2011: a referendum in Wales to approve the granting of additional law-making powers to the Welsh Assembly
- 2011: a referendum to decide whether to adopt the alternative vote (AV) system for general elections in the UK

The fact that the UK Constitution is unentrenched is critical. It means it is not only flexible, but also vulnerable to change by temporary governments which may wish to amend the constitution to suit themselves.

Uncodified constitution A constitution that is not set down in a single, organised document. This means it is to be found in a number of different sources. The UK Constitution is an example.

Examiner tip

Make sure you can describe briefly at least two constitutional statutes, two constitutional conventions and two constitutional referendums to illustrate the sources of the UK Constitution.

It is unitary

Legal sovereignty in the UK lies with the UK Parliament in Westminster. From time to time Parliament may delegate powers elsewhere, but this is not a transfer of sovereignty. The powers granted to the Scottish, Welsh and Northern Irish governments in the devolution process after 1998 can all be restored to the Westminster Parliament or overruled by it. Thus, we say that a good deal of power has been transferred to the national regions and to elected mayors, but no sovereignty has been given up.

It is based on parliamentary sovereignty

The working of the uncodified constitution is dependent on the existence of parliamentary sovereignty. There are a number of reasons why parliamentary sovereignty is critical to how the political system works.

1 The nature of the constitution is in the hands of Parliament. Parliament can amend the constitution by simple passage of a statute.

2 Government owes all its power to the authority of Parliament. A government (or any other public body) can exercise power only if it receives the approval of Parliament.

3 The constitution is unitary (see above).

4 The constitution is not entrenched. Each new parliament (after each election) is able to pass whatever laws it wishes. The constitution is not bound by past parliaments and it cannot bind any future parliaments.

There is no separation of powers

This means that government is not separately elected but is drawn from the parliamentary majority. We say the government is *part of* Parliament. The lack of separation of power also means that Parliament does not control government, but rather supports it.

Constitutional monarchy and prerogative powers

A constitutional monarchy has two main meanings:

1 The monarch has no political power or role.

2 The monarch's arbitrary (uncontrolled) powers are not exercised by the queen (or king) but by the prime minister. These powers include appointing and dismissing ministers, conducting relations with foreign powers and commanding the armed forces.

A strong executive

The UK Constitution gives rise to a relatively strong executive branch (government) and a relatively weak legislature (Parliament). This is a result of:
- the lack of a separation of powers between the two branches
- the electoral system of first-past-the-post, which usually ensures that the government has a majority in the House of Commons (though this was not the case in 2010 — an unusual event when no party won an overall majority)

Parliamentary sovereignty A political principle where legal sovereignty resides in the national parliament and is not shared with any other body. This is a central feature of the UK political system.

Knowledge check 2

Why is parliamentary sovereignty so important in the British political system?

Constitutionalism A term that describes a system of government where the government itself is subject to constitutional rules. The opposite of constitutionalism is arbitrary government. The UK, being a monarchy, has a government that is 'theoretically' arbitrary, but in fact the monarch has no power. Both monarchy and government are subject to constitutional rules, even though the constitution is not codified.

- the extensive arbitrary powers enjoyed by the prime minister (i.e. **prerogative powers**)

Although the legislature is sovereign, it is the executive that initiates most legislation.

The rule of law

The rule of law means:
- all are equal under the law
- all are entitled to fair trial if accused of a crime
- the government itself is subject to laws and cannot exceed them

Sources of the UK Constitution

When a country's constitution is codified, the constitution has one single source — that is, it is *all* contained in one single document. As the UK Constitution is not codified it has a number of different sources. In other words it can be found in a number of different sources. These sources, together with examples, are shown in Table 1.

Table 1 Sources of the UK Constitution

Source	Description	Examples
Parliamentary statutes	Laws passed by the UK Parliament	**The Scotland Act and Wales Acts 1998**, granting devolved powers to those countries **The Human Rights Act 1998**, bringing the European Convention on Human Rights into British law **The Freedom of Information Act 2000**, granting citizens rights to view most official documents
Conventions	Unwritten rules that are generally followed by those involved in government and politics	**The Salisbury Convention**, by which the House of Lords does not obstruct proposals contained in the government's most recent election manifesto **Collective cabinet responsibility**, which establishes that all members of the government must defend all official government policy or resign
Authoritative documents and books	Like conventions, these are books and documents which are not laws but are generally followed	**The 1689 Bill of Rights** that established the sovereignty of Parliament **A.V. Dicey's nineteenth-century rule of law**, establishing that all citizens must be treated equally under the law **Gus O'Donnell Rules (2010)**, stating how government should be formed if there is a hung parliament

Elective dictatorship A description often used for the relationship between the government and Parliament in the UK. It suggests that, once elected, a government has almost dictatorial powers because it dominates Parliament through its majority in the House of Commons.

Source	Description	Examples
Common law	Historic laws, which are enforced by the courts but have not been passed by Parliament	**The royal prerogative**, whereby the arbitrary powers of the monarch are exercised by the prime minister
		Individual rights, other than those covered by the European Convention on Human Rights, being guaranteed by common law
EU treaties	Treaties signed by the UK government and which are binding on future governments	**Maastricht Treaty (1992)**, transferring a good deal of sovereignty from the UK to the EU
Traditions	Historic practices of limited importance	**Parliamentary procedures**, which are customs governing how both Houses of Parliament behave
		The Queen's Speech, which traditionally introduces the government's annual legislative programme

Unitary constitution [1]
A political system where all legal sovereignty is located in one single place. The UK Constitution is a unitary constitution with all legal sovereignty resting with the UK Parliament.

Federal constitution
A political system where legal sovereignty is divided between central and regional institutions. The USA is an example of a federal constitution, where sovereignty is shared between Washington and the 50 states of the Union.

Codified constitution
A constitution that is organised and written down in one single document, usually at one point in history. It also implies that constitutional law is superior to other laws. The constitution of the USA is perhaps the earliest example of a codified constitution.

Unitary and federal constitutions

Unitary constitutions

A **unitary constitution** is one where legal sovereignty lies in one central location. This implies that:
- sovereignty in the UK lies in the Westminster Parliament
- powers may be delegated (or devolved) to local and regional government
- devolved or delegated powers can be taken back by Parliament, or overruled by it

Federal constitutions

Federal constitutions (examples — USA, Germany) have the following features:
- Legal sovereignty is shared between the centre and regional bodies.
- The sovereignty of regional bodies cannot be removed unless there is a constitutional amendment.
- Any legal sovereignty not granted to the central power is automatically given to regional bodies.

The debate about codified and uncodified constitutions

Should the UK have a codified constitution?

YES because:
- it would clarify the nature of the political system after the constitutional changes since 1997 such as devolution and House of Lords reform

- the process of judicial review would be clear and transparent
- it would include clear protections for the rights of citizens
- it might prevent the further drift towards excessive executive power
- it would clarify the UK's relationship with the EU
- it would be clear to all citizens what is, or is not, constitutional
- it would bring the UK into line with most other modern democracies

NO because:

- the current constitution is flexible and can easily be adapted to changing circumstances unlike codified constitutions whose provisions are entrenched and require complicated procedures before they can be amended
- it is not necessary because the current constitution has stood the test of time
- the lack of constitutional restraints allows for strong and decisive government
- a codified constitution would give too much power to unelected judges

Sovereignty

Sovereignty refers to the ultimate power that may be exercised within a state. It may be determined by some form of constitutional settlement, or simply by historical convention. Sovereignty also sets apart the jurisdiction between different states. It may be classified in particular ways. At this level of study, it is useful to distinguish between political sovereignty and legal sovereignty.

Legal sovereignty

Legal sovereignty refers to the idea of 'ultimate' political power which cannot be overruled by any other body or law. It also locates the origin of all political power — that is, who, or what, can grant power to an individual or body. It is called legal sovereignty because it has the force of law and will be enforced by the law courts. Finally, it is also the place where the supreme laws are made. In the UK, the Westminster Parliament is normally regarded as legally sovereign since it is the origin of all power and the place where binding laws are made.

Political sovereignty

The term **political sovereignty** refers to where actual, practical power lies, whoever may make the laws. Political sovereignty could be said to exist in the following places:

- with the people at times of elections
- with the people during a referendum
- with the government when it controls its own majority in the UK Parliament
- with devolved governments (Scotland, Wales, Northern Ireland), since it is almost inconceivable that their powers will be removed

The UK Constitution in the EU context

The implications of UK membership of the EU are as follows:

- The national parliaments of member states cannot overrule EU law. The Factortame case of 1990 first established this principle — the European Court of Justice struck down UK fisheries legislation that ran contrary to EU law.

Examiner tip

Examiners often ask about codified and uncodified constitutions. Remember, though, that much of the UK Constitution is now written, though not in one single place. Also remember that the fact it is not codified makes it very flexible, but flexibility does not *always* make it easy to change. Today, by convention, any major change needs a positive referendum vote.

Knowledge check 3

Where does sovereignty now lie in the UK?

Pooled sovereignty
A situation where the legal sovereignty of one state is shared with the sovereignty of a number of other states. This is how the EU operates. Some legal sovereignty is retained by member states but some sovereignty is granted to the international institution. Thus member states are pooling their sovereignty.

Knowledge check 4

How has the UK lost
sovereignty to the
European Union?

Devolution An
arrangement where
power, but not sovereignty,
is distributed to regional
bodies. Devolved power
can be removed or
overruled by the central
body, so no sovereignty
is transferred. This is
the situation in the UK
where some power has
been devolved to Wales,
Scotland and Northern
Ireland, though the UK
Parliament remains
sovereign.

Examiner tip

Make sure you know
and can express clearly
the difference between
devolution and federalism.
Devolution is the
delegation of power
which can be returned
to Westminster, whereas
federalism means that
sovereignty is distributed
to regions, as in the USA.

Quasi-federalism
Devolution is often
described as 'quasi-
federalism'. This means
that devolution has
the appearance of a
distribution of sovereignty
to regional bodies, but is
not actually federalism in
the true sense of the word.

- However, EU law is currently confined to a limited number of areas. Key policy areas, such as the economy, law and order, welfare, education and foreign affairs, are not covered by EU law.
- Ultimately, of course, the UK can leave the EU if it wishes.
- The UK courts must implement EU law.

Sovereignty and devolution

After the 1997 general election, the Blair government introduced devolution, first for Scotland and Wales and then for Northern Ireland. Devolution involves a large degree of self-government and directly elected national assemblies.

With devolution, sovereignty resides in a central authority, but certain powers are handed down to subnational bodies. The Westminster Parliament retains the right to alter these powers (to remove some of them, for example) or to abolish the subnational bodies entirely. Devolution does not entail any *fixed amount* of power being transferred from the national to subnational level. Indeed, if you look at devolution across the UK, a number of models may be observed, each with different amounts of power.

The location of sovereignty in the UK

As we see above, the location of sovereignty in the UK is not a straightforward question. We can, however, make the following statements:
- Legal sovereignty lies with the UK Parliament at Westminster.
- It can be argued that the government shares legal sovereignty with Parliament.
- Some legal sovereignty has been delegated to the EU but the UK can claim it back by leaving the EU.
- Political sovereignty lies with the people at elections.
- The people also become sovereign when a referendum is held. Though not binding on the UK Parliament, a referendum result would never be ignored.
- The governments of the UK, Scotland, Wales and Northern Ireland all enjoy political sovereignty.
- The location of political sovereignty in the UK may move depending on the relationship between government and Parliament, and depending on changes in the amount of power devolved to Scotland, Wales and Northern Ireland.

Evaluation of the UK Constitution

Table 2 shows the positive elements of the UK's constitutional arrangements alongside some of the main criticisms.

Table 2 The UK Constitution evaluated

Positive elements	Negative elements
It is flexible. Because it is uncodified, it can evolve naturally and respond easily to changing circumstances	It is too flexible and so can be amended by a temporary government that wishes to serve its own purposes
It provides for strong, decisive government which is not constrained by constitutional rules. The government's mandate is normally clear	It allows governments to have too much power as there are inadequate constitutional safeguards in place

Positive elements	Negative elements
It has stood the test of time and so remains part of Britain's political traditions	It is old fashioned and does not conform to the normal picture of a modern constitution. It allows for undemocratic institutions such as the House of Lords and the monarchy
The doctrine of parliamentary sovereignty makes government relatively accountable	Parliament is too weak relative to government and it is insufficiently representative. The electoral system reinforces the lack of representation
Its unitary nature helps to maintain national unity	Power is too centralised and so threatens democracy
The independent judiciary ensures that the rule of law is maintained	Individual rights are not well protected because Parliament is not subject to constitutional control
It provides for a collective form of government, as opposed to presidential systems which may place too much power in the hands of one individual	The fact that the constitution is not codified means that citizens find it difficult to understand

Knowledge check 5

Identify and outline three criticisms of the UK Constitution.

Constitutional reform in the UK

Labour's post-1997 reforms

Following the 1997 general election, in which Labour came to power, a number of reforms to the UK Constitution were implemented.

Devolution for Scotland, Wales and Northern Ireland

Devolution was introduced in Scotland and Wales in 1998 after successful referendums in 1997. Scotland voted for a parliament with tax-varying and primary legislative powers. Wales narrowly voted in favour of an assembly with administrative devolution. In addition, the UK government secured the consent of the people of Northern Ireland for a new devolved assembly in the province in 1998. In 2011, a Welsh referendum voted to grant legislative powers to the Welsh Assembly too.

Examiner tip

Make sure you check what time period the question is asking about. In this case, you may be asked about reform either since 1997 or since 2010.

Human rights legislation

In 1998 the European Convention on Human Rights (ECHR) was incorporated into UK law in the form of the **Human Rights Act** (HRA). For the first time, rights such as freedom of speech and fair trial were written into law. Citizens no longer have to go to the European Court of Human Rights in Strasbourg in order to have their rights protected. The ECHR is binding on all bodies engaged in 'public business'. It can be enforced by the UK law courts (with final appeals going to the European Court of Human Rights).

The HRA is limited because it is *not* binding on the UK Parliament. However, the UK government and Parliament will ignore the ECHR only under exceptional circumstances (such as an outbreak of terrorism), so this is, normally, binding.

The **Freedom of Information Act** (FOIA) was passed in 2000. This gave citizens the right to see documents relating to any public business, as well as information held about themselves. The Act was designed to improve the openness of government and has had a major impact, not least when the inflated expenses claims of many MPs were revealed in 2009–10.

Electoral reform

Changes to the UK's electoral systems have come about either in their own right or in conjunction with other reforms that have taken place. For example, the devolved bodies in Edinburgh, Cardiff and Belfast are all elected using various proportional electoral systems.

Elections to the Greater London Authority are also conducted under a proportional system. The London mayor is elected every 4 years using the supplementary vote system. Since 1999, UK elections to the European Parliament have been run using a version of the party-list system. Before that time, these elections used the simple plurality (first-past-the-post) system.

Elected mayors

Blair's government was keen to introduce US-style, directly elected mayors in some of the UK's major cities. The most important development took place in London. The first elected London mayor — Ken Livingstone — took office in 2000. Referendums have been held in towns such as Doncaster and Hartlepool, and, where there was a 'yes' vote, the newly elected mayors assumed a number of authority-wide strategic powers. By 2011, there were 11 such elected mayors in smaller cities.

Reform of the House of Lords

A limited reform was passed in 1999 when all but 92 of the hundreds of hereditary peers lost their voting rights. Thus, most of the House of Lords was composed of appointed life peers. This gave the Lords a little more democratic legitimacy, but failed to meet demands for an elected element. Further attempts at reform failed until after the 2010 general election.

Reform of the judiciary

In 2005 the Constitutional Reform Act was passed. Its main element was the creation of the Supreme Court. This replaced the system where the highest court of appeal, and therefore the constitutional court, was made up of a selection of 12 judges who were members of the House of Lords. The separated Supreme Court is designed to be more independent from political influences. This, it is hoped, will make it more effective in protecting individual rights and controlling excessive government power. At the same time, it was established that the head of the judiciary should no longer be a member of the government and the appointments system was overhauled to reduce political interference.

The uncompleted elements of the post-1997 reforms

Labour had an ambitious reform programme in 1997, but a good deal of it was never accomplished. The main examples of incomplete reforms were these:

- Reform of the House of Lords was modest and there was no agreement on a fully reformed second chamber.
- Labour had promised to hold a referendum on full-scale electoral reform for general elections. This was never held.
- Labour proposed to introduce devolved assemblies to the English regions, but this policy was destroyed by a negative referendum result in the North East in 2004.

Evaluation of Labour's reforms

Positive aspects of the Labour reforms

Devolution

The Scots and the Welsh are now governed by devolved bodies that are closer to the people and therefore more responsive to their needs. In Scotland it is argued that, as a consequence of the coalition administrations, there is greater consensual politics, based on moderation and agreement.

Human rights legislation

The Human Rights Act has set down for the first time the rights that UK citizens should expect and has brought the UK into line with other European countries. A key criticism of the status of rights in the UK before the introduction of the Act was that they were vulnerable to the whim of Parliament. It was also claimed that a feature of the UK Constitution in the postwar era was the gradual erosion of citizens' rights. This has largely been stemmed. The Freedom of Information Act has had a dramatic effect on the people's and the media's ability to access official information.

Electoral reform

Representatives of smaller parties, such as the Green Party and the UK Independence Party, have won election to the European Parliament because the relationship between votes and seats is more proportional than before. The proportional voting system used for elections to the Scottish Parliament saw the Conservatives gain a fairer representation for their supporters (compared with the outcome of elections for Scottish constituencies in the House of Commons).

House of Lords

Though the composition of the Lords has changed only modestly, there is no doubt that the reformed House has become more active and more professional, taking a more active role in scrutinising proposed legislation and in checking the arbitrary power of government.

Knowledge check 6

Outline three elements of constitutional reform that Labour failed to complete after 1997.

Elected mayors

The introduction of an elected London mayor has been largely successful and popular. London's first two mayors — Livingstone and Boris Johnson — were prominent politicians and have raised the city's profile.

Judicial reform

The Supreme Court, which came into existence in 2009, has proved to be active in protecting individual rights and in scrutinising possible examples of excessive and unjust power being exercised by public bodies.

Criticisms of Labour's reforms

There are two broad fronts of criticism directed at the reforms of Blair's Labour government: that the reforms were inadequate (from the Liberal Democrat perspective) and that the reforms have gone too far (traditionally, the Conservative view).

The reforms were inadequate and incomplete

This is a liberal argument:
- Too much of the programme was not completed, notably electoral reform and the introduction of a more democratic House of Lords. This has led to a great deal of discontent and a feeling that Britain remains fundamentally undemocratic.
- It is also argued that the HRA is inadequate because it is not binding on the UK Parliament. This means that rights remain under threat (notably in the face of anti-terrorism legislation). Many liberals suggest that the only adequate answer will be the introduction of a codified constitution.
- Despite devolution, power in the UK is too centralised.
- The key argument concerns the power of government, which liberals see as excessive. They argue for even more reform of both Houses of Parliament, a stronger Bill of Rights and curbs on the prime minister's power to restore the balance back towards the people and their elected representatives.
- The failure to introduce electoral reform is seen as a major failing. Without electoral reform, it is said, Parliament will never be truly representative.

The reforms went too far

This is an argument presented by traditional Conservatives:
- The Human Rights Act is too much of a constraint on the powers of the government and Parliament. Furthermore, its terms are determined outside the UK, at the Council of Europe, and enforcement is ultimately by a European court.
- The House of Lords is little more than a chamber of political 'placemen' and is not independent enough of party control.
- Devolution has threatened the unity of the UK.
- The Supreme Court puts too much power in the hands of unelected, unaccountable judges.

The 2010 coalition and constitutional reform

The coalition government of 2010 included a range of proposed constitutional reforms as part of its two-party agreement. The reasons why such a programme was proposed are as follows:

- The Liberal Democrats demanded constitutional reform as part of the price of agreeing to support the larger Conservative Party.
- David Cameron portrayed himself as a modern prime minister on the 'liberal wing' of the Conservative Party.
- There was widespread public disillusionment with, and suspicion of, politics in the UK. The reforms were an attempt to restore public confidence in politics.
- Both coalition parties had criticised the outgoing Labour government for failing to complete its reform programme. They therefore made a virtue of completing the reforms started by Labour.

Table 3 shows the proposals of the coalition government. Note that these were the 2010 proposals. Students must bring themselves up to date on when or whether these reforms have been implemented since 2010.

Examiner tip
Always have plenty of examples of constitutional reforms, both before and after 2010, to illustrate your answers on this topic. You should know five examples of reform before 2010 and three after 2010.

Table 3 The 2010 coalition constitutional reform proposals

Proposal	Detail
Electoral reform	A referendum was proposed to decide whether the alternative vote (AV) system should be adopted for Westminster elections. This referendum was held in May 2011 and the proposal was rejected. Electoral reform is therefore off the political agenda for the foreseeable future
Fixed-term parliaments	Agreed in 2010. The gap between elections to the House of Commons was fixed at 5 years. This took away the prime minister's power to determine the date of general elections
House of Lords reform	Legislation to be introduced to create a partly or fully elected House of Lords
A British Bill of Rights	Consideration to be given to replacing the HRA with a British Bill of Rights outside the control of the European Court of Human Rights
Equal constituency sizes	2011 legislation began the process of redrawing constituency boundaries to ensure all parliamentary constituencies are of equal size in terms of population
Recall of MPs	Constituents to have the power to hold a vote on whether to 'recall' MPs who abuse their position
Devolution	Promised a Welsh referendum on more power to its Assembly to be honoured (a 'yes' vote was achieved in February 2011)
	Promised to allow a Scottish referendum on increased powers to the Scottish government and Parliament
European Union	Any proposed transfer of sovereignty to the EU could take place only following a 'yes' vote in a referendum
Elected mayors	Referendums to be held in major cities to determine whether they should introduce elected mayors (if there is not already one in existence)

The Constitution

- The purposes of a political constitution
- The sources of the British Constitution (in what forms can it be found)
- The main features of the British Constitution (what makes it typical and what makes it distinctive)
- Distinctions between unitary and federal constitutions
- Evaluations of how effective and democratic the British Constitution is
- Analysis and evaluation of the arguments for and against codification
- The main constitutional reforms that have taken place, or been proposed, in the UK since 1997

- The reasons why such proposals and reforms were instituted
- Evaluations of how effective reforms have been since 1997
- Knowledge and evaluations of how the British Constitution could be further reformed and improved
- Understanding of key concepts and definitions such as codification, entrenchment, sovereignty and its locations, rule of law, judiciability, separation of powers
- How the British Constitution is affected by membership of the EU

Parliament

The functions of Parliament

Parliament Otherwise known as the legislature. However, Parliament is not merely the central law-making institution. It is also the main way in which citizens are represented; and it controls the power of government, forcing it to be accountable. Above all, Parliament exists to grant formal consent to legislation even though it is dominated by the government.

Note that this section refers only to the UK **Parliament** (i.e. Westminster Parliament). It does not necessarily relate to the Scottish Parliament.

The main functions of the UK Parliament as a whole are as follows:
- **Legislation** It gives formal approval to proposed laws. Most laws (unwritten common law is an exception) will be enforced by the authorities and courts only if they have been passed by Parliament.
- **Scrutiny** It scrutinises proposed laws to ensure they will be clear, effective and fair to different sections of society.
- **Accountability** It calls the government to account, forcing ministers and other officials to explain policies, justify them and listen to criticisms.
- **Representation** It tries to ensure that all parliamentary constituencies and various sections of the whole community are properly represented, seeking to make sure that their interests are taken into account in government decisions.
- **Rights protection** It seeks to protect the rights and freedoms of individual citizens.
- **Redress of grievances** MPs as individuals take up the grievances of individual citizens who feel they have been unfairly treated by a public body. This is known as the redress of grievances.
- **Deliberation** It may debate and deliberate on the great issues of the day, such as the conduct of military action by British forces, the direction of British foreign policy or moral and religious matters.

Distinctions between the House of Commons and the House of Lords

A key distinction to be made between the House of Commons and the House of Lords is that the former is elected whereas the latter is unelected.

Further distinctions can be made in terms of the functions of the two Houses. These are shown in Table 4.

Table 4 Distinctions between the functions of the House of Commons and House of Lords

Shared functions	House of Commons only	House of Lords only
Granting formal consent to legislation	Granting popular consent to proposed legislation	Deliberating at length on important issues
Calling government to account	Refusing to approve items of legislation which are undesirable	Providing specialist, expert advice on proposed legislation
Scrutinising proposed legislation and amending it where necessary	Representing the interests of constituencies	Delaying legislation (but not vetoing it), forcing government to reconsider
Debating key issues	Bringing attention to the grievances of individual constituents	
Representing the interests of different sections of society		

Knowledge check 7

Distinguish between the functions of the House of Commons and those of the House of Lords.

Composition and structure of the House of Commons

The House of Commons is made up of the following main components:

- **650 Members of Parliament** Each Member of Parliament (MP) is elected by a constituency. In the Westminster Parliament there are constituencies in England, Scotland, Wales and Northern Ireland. (Note that 650 was the number in 2011 — this may change.)
- **Frontbench MPs** These are prominent members of the political parties who tend to sit (as their name suggests) on the benches in the centre of the chamber in front of all the other MPs. Frontbenchers are made up of ministers in the government (normally about 80) and leading members of the other parties (normally about 30). Note that all ministers and other frontbenchers are elected by constituencies (even the prime minister) and so are also MPs. They have a dual role.
- **Backbench MPs** Backbenchers are all the other MPs who do not have a ministerial post and/or who are not senior members of their party.
- **The speaker** The speaker of the House of Commons is elected by all MPs and must become politically neutral. He or she chairs the Commons, keeping order and organising the business of the House in conjunction with the party leaderships. The speaker is also concerned with the conduct of MPs and may discipline them.
- **Legislative committees** These are formed for each proposed piece of legislation. They contain between 15 and 40 backbench MPs. Their task is to examine proposed laws and to put forward amendments which may improve the legislation. Such amendments require the approval of the whole House of Commons.

- **Departmental select committees** These committees are permanent and normally contain 11–13 members. In 2011 there were 19 of these committees. Their chairs are elected by backbench MPs. They examine the work of government departments, checking for efficiency, value for money, desirable policy making etc. They may criticise (or praise) departments in their regular reports.
- **Public accounts committee** This is a select committee that examines government finances. It seeks to ensure that money is spent on purposes approved by Parliament and that money is not wasted. The PAC also concerns itself with the interests of taxpayers and those who receive government financial support.
- **Whips offices** Whips are appointed by the three main parties. They are respected MPs whose role is to inform MPs about the business of the House, ensure that MPs turn up when required and maintain party discipline, trying to ensure that all MPs will support their party's official policies. They also keep the frontbenchers aware of the 'mood' of their party's backbench MPs and try to head off potential rebellions.

The Westminster model This concept suggests that Parliament is the centre of the political system. It is now seen as outdated, as the centre of power lies with the prime minister and the government.

Party make-up of the Commons

Table 5 shows the parties to which the 650 MPs belonged in the Parliament of 2010.

Table 5 Seats in the House of Commons, 2010

Party	Seats
Conservative	305
Labour	255
Liberal Democrat	57
Democratic Unionist	8
Scottish National	6
Sinn Fein	4
Plaid Cymru	3
Social Democratic & Labour	3
Alliance	1
Green	1
Independent	2
Speaker and three deputies	4
Vacant (Belfast West)	1
Total number of seats	**650**

Representative and responsible government
A description of the British political system, this asserts that the people are represented through parties and Parliament and that the government is made responsible to the people through Parliament.

The Conservative–Liberal Democrat coalition has a total of 362 MPs. Other parties have a total of 288 MPs.

Composition and structure of the House of Lords

The House of Lords is not elected, so its composition is not as straightforward as that of the House of Commons. The following types of peer are members of the House of Lords. Note that the numbers were correct in March 2011 but may have changed since then.

- **Life peers (630)** Individuals who are appointed as peers and therefore members of the House of Lords. Attendance is not compulsory and some rarely attend. Most are active members of a political party, but many are neutral and are known as crossbenchers.
- **Hereditary peers (92)** These are a remnant of a past age when most members of the House of Lords were hereditary peers. Since 1999 their number has been reduced to 92. Hereditary peers have inherited their title by being the eldest son of a member of the aristocracy who has died. Some have a political allegiance, many do not and are therefore also crossbenchers.
- **Archbishops and bishops of the Church of England (26)** Because the Church of England is known as the 'established' church of the UK, its senior bishops and archbishops are entitled to sit in the Lords.
- **The Lord Speaker** Carries out similar functions to the speaker of the Commons.

The Lords has the following main structure:
- **Frontbench peers** These are the equivalent of the frontbench MPs in the Commons but there are considerably fewer of them (about 20 government frontbenchers and less for the other parties).
- **Backbench peers** All peers who are not on the front benches.
- **Public bill committees** Composed of between 12 and 16 members for each piece of proposed legislation, these committees examine legislation and propose amendments to improve the legislation. Any amendments must be approved by the House of Commons.
- **Whips offices** Whips in the House of Lords have a similar role to those in the Commons, though they have considerably less influence and fewer means to discipline peers who defy their party line. Neutral, crossbench peers are not subject to whips.

The political make-up of the House of Lords

Table 6 gives a breakdown of the peers by political allegiance in March 2011.

Table 6 Party allegiance in the House of Lords, 2011

Allegiance	Peers
Conservative	219
Labour	242
Liberal Democrat	94
Crossbench (non-political)	183
Bishops (non-political)	26

Thus, in 2011, 313 peers were government supporters, while 451 supported other parties or were non-political.

Examiner tip
You should know the party make-up of both Houses of Parliament, though not necessarily the exact numbers. Make sure you keep up to date as the numbers do change.

Parliamentary committees

Much of the work of both Houses of Parliament is done in committees — groups of MPs and/or peers who have a specialised function. There are many types of committee. In Table 7 we evaluate the most important ones which are relevant to examination questions:

Table 7 Evaluation of committees

Committee	Strengths	Weaknesses
House of Commons departmental select committees	They act largely independently of party control They have power to call ministers, civil servants and outsiders as witnesses to their hearings They may call for official documents They are given time for extensive questioning and investigation They are respected by policy makers	They have relatively little research back-up They have no ability to enforce their recommendations They are sometimes put under pressure by party whips to take a particular view. They are not *always* independent
House of Commons public accounts committee (PAC)	Has always acted independently. The chair is, by tradition, an opposition MP It has full access to details of government financial arrangements It is highly respected by policy makers	It cannot enforce its recommendations
House of Commons legislative committees (mostly public bill committees)	They have the opportunity to examine legislation in detail	They nearly always divide on party lines and so are not independent They lack expertise and research back-up If they take too much time, the government can curtail their debates Their decisions may be overturned by the whole House
House of Lords public bill committees	Many members have specialist knowledge, experience and expertise They are relatively independent and free of party control They can be obstructive and so gain concessions from the government	Their proposed amendments can be overturned in the House of Commons The government can re-present proposed legislation in the next parliamentary session, in which case committees are powerless to interfere

Knowledge check 8

Distinguish between the role of select and legislative committees of Parliament.

The relationship between government and Parliament

The key to analysing the behaviour and functioning of Parliament lies in its relationship to the government of the day. It is also important to note that this relationship is different depending on whether it is between the government and the House of Commons or between the government and the House of Lords. The key facts about this relationship are as follows:

House of Commons

Factors in the government's favour

- It is normal for the government to enjoy the support of a majority of MPs in the Commons. In the past, this has been because the governing party has won an overall majority of the available seats at a general election (for example, 326 seats in a House of 650 members). In 2010, no single party won such an overall majority and so the Conservatives and Liberal Democrats formed a coalition which could command such a majority jointly.
- Patronage is an important factor. Most MPs hope, one day, to be promoted to ministerial office. To achieve this they need to demonstrate to the prime minister (who appoints all ministers) that they are loyal party members.
- The government whips have a number of methods by which they can persuade their own party's MPs to support the government, even if they have reservations.
- In the legislative committees that consider possible amendments to legislation, the government side is always granted a majority of its own MPs.
- The government controls most of the timetable of the Commons. This makes it possible for it to cut short (even avoid) debates which might embarrass it.

Factors in the House of Commons' favour

- Ultimately the Commons can vote against a government proposal, either a whole bill or an amendment to a bill.
- The departmental select committees (see above under 'composition and structure of the House of Commons' and also Table 7) tend to act independently of MPs' party allegiances. The reports of these committees can often be critical and can force changes in government policy.
- Government must make itself accountable to the House of Commons. This means MPs have ample opportunities to criticise the government and to publicise its shortcomings.

House of Lords

Factors in the government's favour

- The Lords has more limited powers than the Commons. Under terms of the **Parliament Act 1949**, it cannot interfere with any measure involving the public

Presidential government The political principle that a president has a separate source of authority from that of the rest of the government.

The separation and fusion of powers The separation of powers is the principle that the powers of the government and Parliament should be separated and that they should each control each other's power. The fusion of powers is where there is no separation between government and Parliament.

Parliamentary government The principle that the government draws its authority from Parliament and not directly from the electorate. This is the principle that characterises the British system. It also means there is no separation between the executive (government) and the legislature (Parliament). The government is part of Parliament and all ministers are drawn from Parliament.

Bicameralism Literally, this means 'two chambers'. It is used to describe a legislature that is divided into two houses. In the case of the UK, these are the Commons and the Lords.

finances and it can only delay proposed legislation for 1 year (and cannot veto it). Any amendments proposed in the Lords must be approved by the Commons. This means that the government can block most (though not all) such amendments.

- The **Salisbury Convention** (an unwritten principle of the UK Constitution) establishes that the House of Lords should not obstruct any legislation which was proposed in the most recent election manifesto of the governing party or parties.
- The government maintains a great deal of control over the business of the House of Lords and so can manipulate the timetable to avoid obstruction or embarrassment.
- There are no departmental select committees in the Lords, so there is less independent examination of the government's decisions, policies and administration.

Factors in the House of Lords' favour

- The government does not enjoy the party support of a majority in the Lords.
- Most members of the Lords (peers) are not professional politicians. This means they can be independent minded.
- The House of Lords cannot veto proposals but can delay and obstruct them. This gives the Lords some influence over the government.
- Many peers have a vast experience in various walks of life such as government, business, finance, trade unionism, medicine, education, the law, religion and military affairs. Many peers also represent large, influential groups in society.

Examiner tip
The nature of the relationship between government and Parliament is central to most questions about Parliament. Make sure you have mastered it.

Evaluation of the House of Commons

This section considers how effectively the House of Commons carries out its roles. The evaluation is best considered in terms of each of those roles in turn.

Representation

Positive

Most MPs are active in representing the interests of their constituencies and of individual constituents. Many MPs also represent the interests of large associations and pressure groups.

Negative

The Commons is not socially representative. Women are in the minority and there are few representatives from minority ethnic groups or from smaller religions. The members are predominantly middle class and from a background in the professions. Party loyalty also means they tend to toe the party line rather than representing national or group interests. The worst aspect is that the party make-up of the Commons does not represent accurately support for the parties among the electorate. Large parties tend to be over-represented, while small parties are under-represented. This is the result of the first-past-the-post electoral system.

Calling government to account

Positive

MPs regularly question ministers at question-time sessions. The **Liaison Committee** also questions the prime minister twice a year. Ministers are forced, by tradition, to present all policies to the Commons before making any other public announcements. The departmental select committees are extremely active and independent. They examine government business closely and are often critical to good effect.

Negative

Prime Minister's Question Time (PMQT) has become something of a media sideshow with little relevance to real policy examination. Many MPs are also reluctant to be critical of ministers of their own party for fear of being seen as disloyal.

Scrutiny

Positive

The departmental select committees have proved to be effective in scrutinising the policies of government departments and publicising shortcomings or failures.

Negative

MPs are given relatively little time to scrutinise proposed legislation, so it is often the case that laws are poorly drafted. Because the legislative committees are whipped into party loyalty, MPs are not independent minded in their scrutiny function.

Legislating

Positive

It is a key role of the Commons to make legislation *legitimate*. This means granting consent on behalf of the people. On the whole this operates well and the laws are generally respected because they have been legitimised in Parliament. The Commons does retain the power to block legislation which is against the public interest or which represents an abuse of power.

Negative

The procedures of Parliament in respect of passing legislation are ancient and considered to be inefficient and ritualised.

Deliberation

Positive

From time to time the Commons is seen at its best in debates on the great issues of the day. Examples include debates on the war in Iraq, over how to deal with terrorism and on the funding of higher education.

Accountability The principle that government should be accountable for its actions. Between elections, this is achieved through Parliament. It means the government must justify its policies and decisions, accept criticism and answer questions put to it by MPs and peers.

Negative

The Commons is given relatively little time for debate on legislation itself, so crowded is its programme. Furthermore, debates on legislative proposals tend to divide along party lines and so lose their authority.

Checking government power

Positive

The Commons retains the power to veto legislation and this represents a discipline upon governments.

Negative

Party loyalty and discipline means that many MPs are reluctant to challenge the government. The government rarely loses a major vote in the Commons.

Knowledge check 9

How does the government control the House of Commons?

Evaluation of the House of Lords

This section considers how effectively the House of Lords carries out its roles. The evaluation is best considered in terms of each of those roles in turn.

Representation

Positive

In many ways the Lords is more representative than the Commons. Many sections of society and associations are represented by peers who have special links with them and specific experience and knowledge.

Negative

The Lords is unelected and so could be said to represent no one because it is not accountable. It is not socially representative, with a high average age, a shortage of women and ethnic minority members and few members from working-class origins.

Calling government to account

Positive

Peers are more independent minded than MPs and can be more active in their questioning and criticisms of ministers.

Negative

There are no departmental select committees in the Lords, so a valuable means by which government can be called to account is missing.

Scrutiny

Positive

The legislative committees in the Lords can be more effective than their counterparts in the Commons. These committees divide much less along party lines and are more independent. Furthermore, the peers who are members of these committees often have special knowledge, expertise and experience in the matters contained in the legislation.

Negative

Though the Lords often does propose legislative amendments, it cannot force them through as they may be overturned by the Commons.

Legislating

Positive

Laws must go through the House of Lords to be passed. There is therefore knowledge that legislation has been fully scrutinised.

Negative

As an unelected body, the Lords cannot provide legitimation to legislation.

Deliberation

Positive

The House of Lords has two great advantages in deliberating on important issues. First, it has more time to do so than the Commons. Second, the Lords contains a vast well of knowledge and experience among its members.

Negative

The fact that the Lords has weak legislating powers means that its debates may be largely symbolic.

Checking government power

Positive

As its members cannot be controlled by the government, the Lords does, from time to time, act in a very independent way.

Negative

The government has several ways of bypassing obstruction by the Lords. The elected government and House of Commons will ultimately win out over the unelected Lords.

Knowledge check 10

Account for the weakness of the House of Lords.

Reform of the House of Commons

Recent reform

In 2010 two reforms were introduced and the coalition government produced proposals for a further four.

The 2010 reforms

- In June 2010 the **Backbench Business Committee** was set up with a chair elected by MPs. The committee controls the debates in the main chamber on 27 days per year and may select any topic. Topics in 2010 included the war in Afghanistan and the concept of the 'big society'. The committee also schedules 8 days of debate in Westminster Central Hall.
- From 2010 onwards the chairs of the departmental select committees are elected by backbench MPs. This takes that power away from the party whips and leaders.

The 2010 proposed reforms

- A House Business Committee is to be set up. This will control the day-to-day business of the House.
- The constituency boundaries are to be redrawn to make them of equal size in terms of population. The ideas behind this reform are that elections will be fairer and MPs will have equal responsibilities.
- Constituents are to be given the power to recall their MPs if they feel there has been an abuse of power or other misconduct. A petition would force a by-election at which the sitting MP would have to seek re-election.
- The size of the House is to be reduced by 10%. This is partly a money-saving measure but will also help to streamline the Commons.

Note that students must bring themselves up to date on which of the proposed reforms are implemented.

> **Examiner tip**
> Make sure you know all four of the reforms proposed by the coalition government in 2010. Also, keep up to date with new developments.

Other proposals

In addition to the above, other proposals have been put forward which may or may not be implemented in the future:

- The key change would have been the reform of the voting system to AV, to be decided by referendum in May 2011 (known as an *external* reform). AV would ensure all MPs were elected by an overall majority of first and subsequent choice votes. This would give them more legitimacy. It would also probably make hung parliaments more common. In the event, the proposal was rejected, setting back any prospect of electoral reform for quite some time to come.
- There have been calls for select and perhaps legislative committees to examine proposed laws *before* they are debated in the House. This would save time and possibly improve the quality of legislation.

- Some have argued for a more streamlined procedure for the passage of legislation, possibly by cutting out one or two of the three main stages by which a bill is debated.

Reform of the House of Lords

The Lords was last reformed in 1999. In that year, all but 92 of the hereditary peers lost their attendance and voting rights. By the time of the 2010 general election, all three main parties were committed to further reform. Proposals were included in the coalition agreement between the Conservatives and Liberal Democrats.

Table 8 provides an evaluation of the various reform proposals.

Table 8 House of Lords reform: proposals and evaluation

Reform	Advantages	Disadvantages
Abolition	It would save money It would streamline the legislative process It would remove obstructions to efficient government It would force the House of Commons to face up to its responsibilities	An important check on governmental power would be lost It would deny many worthy individuals the opportunity to engage in politics The expertise of the second chamber would be lost
All appointed	Many useful, knowledgeable individuals could be brought in to politics It would be an opportunity to manipulate the membership to ensure a political and social balance It would result in a more independent body than an elected chamber	It might put too much patronage power into the hands of party leaders
Fully elected	It is the most democratic solution Members would be fully accountable The House would have more authority and so be a more effective check on governmental power If elected by proportional representation, it would reflect the strengths of the parties more accurately	The House might become too influential and so obstruct the government excessively It might be unnecessary to have two elected chambers The people might be apathetic if faced by too many elections
Mixed elected and appointed	It would enjoy the advantages of both the main alternatives	It would suffer from the same problems as the two main alternatives

Knowledge check 11

Why is House of Commons reform so important?

Knowledge check 12

Why is House of Lords reform so controversial?

Examiner tip

Make sure you keep up to date with the debate on House of Lords reform, including any proposed legislation.

Parliament

- The roles of Parliament
- The structure of both Houses of Parliament
- Knowledge and analysis of representation in Parliament
- Key distinctions between the House of Commons and the House of Lords
- Understanding and analysis of the role of parliamentary committees

- Evaluation of the effectiveness of both Houses, individually or collectively
- Understanding of the relationship between government and Parliament
- Understanding and evaluation of the representative role of Parliament (both Houses)
- Understanding and evaluation of past or proposed reforms of the House of Commons
- Understanding and evaluation of past or proposed reforms of the House of Lords

The prime minister and cabinet

The nature and role of the cabinet

The nature of the cabinet

The cabinet in Britain has the following characteristics:

- It is composed of between 20 and 25 senior politicians, all appointed directly by the prime minister.
- Members of the cabinet must be members of either the House of Commons (i.e. they are MPs) or the House of Lords (i.e. peers).
- Normally one party wins an overall majority of the seats in the Commons and so forms a government alone. In this case *all* members of the cabinet will be from that governing party.
- Where, as in 2010, there is a coalition, the members of cabinet can be from either or all of the parties in the coalition. In 2010, therefore, there were both Conservative and Liberal Democrat members of the cabinet.
- Cabinet meets normally once a week, more often if there is a crisis or emergency.
- The prime minister normally chairs the meetings. Together with the **cabinet secretary,** the most senior civil servant, the prime minister decides what will be discussed in the cabinet and notes in the minutes (the detailed accounts of meetings) what was decided.
- A number of **cabinet committees** are created to deal in detail with specific areas of government policy. These have a small number of members (perhaps between four and six) and will be chaired by the prime minister or another senior cabinet member. Typical examples are defence, foreign affairs, environment, education, health.

Cabinet government
A principle whereby the cabinet is the centre of policy making and is the central decision-making institution. It also implies that the prime minister may have higher status than the cabinet but that he or she must seek its approval for all policies.

- The minutes of the cabinet meetings remain a secret for at least 30 years. However, the main cabinet decisions are made widely known.
- Cabinet decisions are, in effect, official government policy.
- The prime minister has the power to dismiss ministers from the cabinet, to appoint new cabinet ministers, to create new cabinet posts or abolish old ones, and may move ministers around into different posts (known as a 'reshuffle').
- The cabinet works on the basis of **collective responsibility** (see below).

The role of the cabinet

- It formalises and legitimises official government policy.
- It sometimes deals with disputes between different government departments and ministers when their proposals conflict or when there are problems allocating scarce government funds between different uses.
- It may meet in special session to deal with a crisis or emergency situation. There was, for example, a series of meetings to formulate a response to the banking and financial crisis which affected the UK in 2007–9.
- Cabinet is where the presentation of policy is determined. This is to ensure that ministers coordinate the way in which policy is portrayed to the media and the public.
- The business of Parliament is arranged in the cabinet in conjunction with the party whips.
- Policy formulation rarely takes place in cabinet, but from time to time the prime minister may invite the whole cabinet to discuss an important issue of the day. The decision to bid for the 2012 Olympics was decided in cabinet, as has been the future of energy policy.

Collective responsibility

The operation of the cabinet depends on the doctrine of collective responsibility. This principle (an unwritten constitutional convention) has the following features:

- All members of the government — including cabinet ministers and junior ministers who are not cabinet members — are collectively responsible for all cabinet decisions and policies.
- All ministers must support and defend cabinet decisions publicly, whether or not they privately disagree.
- A minister who breaks with collective responsibility is expected to resign (see Table 9) or, if not, will probably be dismissed by the prime minister.
- In a coalition, ministers may disagree with official policy in public, but once a cabinet decision is reached they are expected to vote with the government in Parliament. However, there have been 'agreements to differ', where even ministers have been able to abstain (not vote at all) on an issue. This happened over the raising of higher education tuition fees in England and Wales in 2010.

Core executive A description of the central core of government where decision making and policy making take place. It also refers to the place where policy is implemented and its presentation determined. It is generally considered to comprise the prime minister, the cabinet, cabinet committees, government departments, the senior civil service and political advisers and policy committees.

Collective responsibility The doctrine that all members of a government are collectively responsible for all its decisions. This also means that all members of government must defend government policy in public, even if they disagree privately. If they cannot support policy, they must resign or expect dismissal.

Knowledge check 13

For what reasons is the doctrine of collective responsibility so important?

Table 9 Resignations from cabinet over collective responsibility

Ministers and dates of resignation	Issue
Robin Cook (Foreign Secretary), 2003 John Denham (Home Office minister), 2003	The decision to support the US-led invasion of Iraq
Clare Short (International Development Secretary), 2003	Post-Iraq war policies
James Purnell (Work and Pensions Secretary), 2009	The general direction of policy under Gordon Brown's leadership
Lee Scott (junior ministerial aide), 2010 Mike Crockart (junior ministerial aide), 2010	The decision to allow universities to increase tuition fees

Prime ministerial power

The sources of prime ministerial power

The prime minister's powers derive from the following sources:

- He or she enjoys **prerogative powers**. In other words, the powers of the monarch as head of state are now exercised by the prime minister in her place. These are:
  - to command and direct the armed forces
  - to conduct foreign policy negotiations and sign treaties
  - to appoint and dismiss government ministers
  - to nominate individuals for peerages
  - to approve the appointment of senior judges and Church of England bishops
  - to speak on behalf of the nation to the media and the people
- He or she is leader of the governing party. Because the governing party (or coalition) has 'won' the most recent election, that party has the right to form the government. As leader of that party, the prime minister is acknowledged to be the senior policy maker and controller of government appointments.
- He or she has some **elective authority** in that he or she can claim to be the leader of the party that has won a popular election.
- He or she enjoys the authority of Parliament. The prime minister leads his or her party, not just in the country, but also in Parliament.

The prime minister's powers

Table 10 distinguishes between the formal and informal powers of the prime minister.

- **Formal powers** are those that derive from the prime minister's being head of state and enjoying prerogative powers. Formal powers do not vary.
- **Informal powers** vary according to the political circumstances of each prime minister. All holders of the office have these powers, but not in equal measure.

Knowledge check 14

For what reasons are prerogative powers so important?

Table 10 The formal and informal powers of the prime minister (PM)

Formal powers	Informal powers
To negotiate foreign treaties	The PM is chief policy maker for the government
To command the armed forces	
To appoint or dismiss ministers	The PM represents the nation to foreign powers
To determine the structure of government and the responsibilities of ministries	The PM controls the business of the cabinet
As head of the civil service, the power to determine its structure	The PM can make decisions which are required to deal with a short-term emergency situation
To grant peerages and appoint people to important public posts	

See the section below for the limitations to prime ministerial power.

The relationship between the prime minister and the cabinet

There are two competing models of British government:

- **Prime ministerial government** This suggests that the prime minister is dominant, controls the cabinet and the whole policy-making process.
- **Cabinet government** This implies that the cabinet remains the centre of power and the main source of policy making. Though the prime minister is the senior member, ultimately the cabinet controls all policy.

How the prime minister can control the cabinet

There is a variety of ways in which the prime minister can manipulate or influence the way cabinet operates and the decisions it reaches. Among them are the following:

- **Patronage** All ministers are appointed by the prime minister and can be dismissed by him or her. The PM can also reshuffle them, sometimes promoting or demoting them.
- **Control of the cabinet agenda** The PM decides what is brought to cabinet. This gives him or her an opportunity to control the making of policy (though not completely — ministers can insist on an agenda item).
- **Bilateral agreements** These are arrangements made by the prime minister with individual ministers or groups of ministers *outside* the main cabinet. Under Tony Blair, it was said these meetings took place on the sofa of his private office and so the practice became known as 'sofa government'.
- **Collective responsibility** It underpins prime ministerial control. Because ministers must accept official government policy, the prime minister can expect their loyalty. Rebellious ministers put their careers in jeopardy.
- **Use of inner cabinets** An inner cabinet is a group of very senior ministers who are close to the prime minister. Members of such a group can control cabinet by determining policy among themselves.

Examiner tip
When answering questions about the prime minister, make sure you can add examples by way of illustration from the experience of the last four prime ministers.

Prime ministerial government A theory that the prime minister dominates the political system. It therefore implies that other bodies in the core executive, notably the cabinet, have a subordinate role.

The limitations to prime ministerial power

Permanent limitations

- The cabinet has the power to overrule a prime minister. The prime minister is limited by the knowledge that he or she must carry the cabinet with him or her.
- The ruling party could remove a prime minister. Though this has not occurred in recent history (with the possible exception that it was pressure from the membership that led to Tony Blair's premature resignation in 2007), the prime minister needs to be careful to maintain the support of his or her party membership.
- Parliament can overrule a prime minister by digging in its heels in opposition to a policy of the prime minister.
- The electorate can bring an end to a prime minister's position. The prime minister will have to face re-election eventually and so must take public opinion into account.

Variable limitations

Here we identify factors which may weaken a specific prime minister. Table 11 shows what limitations afflicted the last four British prime ministers.

Table 11 Factors limiting prime ministerial power since 1990

Prime minister	Limiting factors
John Major (1990–97)	He led a disunited party, split over Britain's relationship with the EU. He could not rely on his cabinet's support
	He started with a small parliamentary majority which was reduced to nothing by 1996
	He had a poor media image, being portrayed as boring and weak
	There was a major economic recession in his first few years in office. This was exacerbated by a run on the pound that humiliated Britain internationally
Tony Blair (1997–2007)	He suffered a disastrous loss of support and confidence after the Iraq war when the war was discovered to be unjustified under international law
	His media image deteriorated, with his being portrayed as obsessed with image and presentation ('spin')
	He was placed under increasing pressure by a faction in the party that supported Gordon Brown for the leadership
Gordon Brown (2007–10)	He suffered from the financial crisis of 2007–9, an event largely outside his control
	He had a poor public and media image, being seen as dull and obsessive
	He endured the threat of an opposition group that campaigned for his removal. He could not rely on the support of all his ministers
David Cameron (2010–)	He inherited a huge problem over the government's financial deficit and so was limited in his policy options
	With no parliamentary majority, he had to form a coalition with the Liberal Democrats. He is limited by the need to maintain Lib Dem support

Examiner tip

When evaluating the limitations on prime ministerial power, make sure you explain the difference between limitations which *all* prime ministers face and those which only *some* prime ministers are confronted with, depending on circumstances. Also, make sure you have examples of these limitations from the experience of recent prime ministers.

We can summarise these variable limitations thus:

- adverse events
- a small or non-existent parliamentary majority for the PM's party
- internal party opposition
- unfavourable media image
- negative public image

What factors does a prime minister take into account when appointing cabinet ministers?

Individual considerations

Individual considerations are particular qualities or circumstances associated with specific people that might make them suitable for promotion to the cabinet. Examples include:

- a close ally of the prime minister (e.g. George Osborne)
- a reward for support in the past (e.g. Oliver Letwin)
- a representative of a significant section of the party, such as a right-wing or left-wing group (e.g. Theresa May)
- in a coalition government, the need to include key figures from the coalition partner's party (e.g. Nick Clegg)
- a potential rebel — because of collective responsibility, including such a potential opponent can be an effective way of silencing them (e.g. Vince Cable)
- simply being foreseen by the prime minister as an effective minister, able to manage a department and implement policy successfully (e.g. David Willetts)

Examiner tip
When discussing cabinet building, make sure you can quote specific examples from the current cabinet.

Team considerations

Most prime ministers prefer a cabinet which is ideologically united and has no major political divisions.

- **Political balance** A politically balanced cabinet means that there will be members from different sections of the party. John Major, in the 1992–97 government, ensured that both the right wing and moderate sections of the party had representatives in the cabinet.
- **Coalition cabinet** In the case of the 2010 coalition government, there was a need to balance the cabinet between the two parties in power. David Cameron chose 18 Conservatives and five Liberal Democrats.
- **Social balance** In a socially balanced cabinet, women or members of ethnic minorities, for example, may be represented to achieve a measure of balance.

Individual ministerial responsibility

Ministers may resign under the principle of *individual* **ministerial responsibility**. This has a number of features:

- Ministers are responsible for all policies and decisions which come under the responsibility of their government department. This is true whether or not they have been directly concerned with a decision or policy.

Individual ministerial responsibility The doctrine that each government minister is personally responsible for all policies and decisions made by his or her department and will be required to resign if an important error is made. It also means that individual ministers should resign over serious examples of personal misconduct.

- On a general level it means that ministers must answer to Parliament for the activities of their department. They must justify their decisions to MPs or peers, accept criticism and explain the reasons behind their actions.
- In extreme circumstances, a minister may be forced to resign if he or she comes under heavy criticism.
- Ministers may also be forced to resign over their personal conduct or concerns over that conduct.

Table 12 gives examples of ministerial resignations since 1998

Table 12 Ministerial resignations

Minister and date	Reasons
Peter Mandelson (Northern Ireland Secretary), 1998	Embarrassing questions over a loan from another party member
Estelle Morris (Education Secretary), 2002	Her own admitted inability to deal with difficult education decisions
David Blunkett (Home Secretary), 2004	Questions over his department's role in possibly interfering with a visa application for a friend's nanny
Shahid Malik (Justice Minister), 2009	Questions over his expenses claims for housing (later overturned and he was re-instated)
Jacqui Smith (Home Secretary), 2010	Revelation of allegations that she had claimed expenses for hiring videos on behalf of her husband
David Laws (Chief Treasury Secretary), 2010	Alleged financial irregularities

Is the British prime minister now effectively a president?

Whether the British prime minister is now effectively a president is a different question to an evaluation of the extent of, and limitations to, the prime minister's power. This question asks whether the power and authority of modern prime ministers has grown so much that he or she is in effect a head of state.

Evidence of presidentialism

- The prime minister enjoys prerogative powers (see above). These are powers that the PM can exercise without the sanction of cabinet or Parliament. They are, therefore, similar to the powers enjoyed by an elected president.
- Michael Foley, an academic commentator, describes a tendency to 'spatial leadership'. This implies that modern prime ministers have tended to separate themselves from the rest of the government. Sometimes they have even criticised

government itself, suggesting that they stand above it. It also means that prime ministers have claimed a direct link to the nation, above the heads of the rest of government.

- The media increasingly treat the prime minister as a quasi-president.
- Several modern prime ministers have adopted a presidential style. This means that they often claim to speak for the nation as a whole (as a president can do), especially during times of crisis.
- Since the 1980s and the end of the Cold War in 1990, prime ministers have increasingly become involved with foreign policy. This has been especially true in terms of the Middle East, the Balkans and parts of Africa.
- There has been a huge growth in the availability of independent advice to the prime minister. There is now an extensive Downing Street machine that looks increasingly like elements of the White House in Washington.
- The personalisation of politics has increased. During elections, the party leaders have become the key figures (notably in the 2010 election with the arrival of televised leadership debates).
- The decline of cabinet has enhanced the power of the prime minister. Cabinet meets less often, for shorter periods, and is less of a collective body than it used to be.

Counter-evidence to the theory of presidentialism

- The prime minister is *not* the head of state, even if he or she behaves like one sometimes.
- The PM does *not* have a separate electoral mandate. He or she is prime minister through being the leader of the largest party, not through being elected separately as PM.
- There are powerful forces that can control the power of the prime minister. These are mainly the cabinet and Parliament. A president has similar checks, but these are not as significant as they are in Britain.
- Not all prime ministers wish to adopt a presidential style of leadership. They may wish to be more consensual, treating government as a collective body and not the instrument of his or her personal power.
- Presidentialism may be merely style rather than substance. This means that a prime minister may *appear* to be a president, but in reality his or her position is different.

To illustrate the above theories about presidentialism, Table 13 details the relevant experience of the two most recent British prime ministers.

Presidentialism
A theory that the power and status of the prime minister has grown so much that he or she is effectively a president or head of state even though he or she remains, in constitutional terms, only head of government.

Knowledge check 16
Distinguish between a head of government and a head of state.

Table 13 Presidentialism and British prime ministers

Prime minister	Factors pointing to or against presidentialism
Tony Blair (1997–2007)	*Positives*
	He led a new political movement — New Labour
	He built up a large policy-making machine reporting to him personally
	He committed the armed forces to four major actions — in Kosovo, Sierra Leone, Iraq and Afghanistan
	He became an important, well-respected world statesman
	He significantly weakened the cabinet and developed much policy personally
	Negatives
	He was ultimately driven out of office by his party colleagues
	He lost his authority at home after the Iraq war
Gordon Brown (2007–10)	*Positives*
	He assumed a dominant personal leadership position during the financial crisis of 2007–9
	He was respected abroad for his handling of financial crisis
	Negatives
	His personal standing in the country began quite low and steadily declined
	He was limited by a divided cabinet
	He did not adopt a presidential 'style'

Knowledge check 17

How have recent British prime ministers become more presidential?

Knowledge summary

The prime minister and cabinet

- Knowledge and understanding of the roles of the prime minister and of the cabinet
- Knowledge and analysis of the sources of prime ministerial power
- Knowledge and understanding of the powers of the prime minister and the limitations to those powers
- Analysis and evaluation of the changing role and power of the prime minister (including knowledge of the experience of prime ministers since 1979)
- Assessment of the importance of the cabinet and limitations to its power and importance
- Knowledge and analysis of collective responsibility and individual ministerial responsibility

- Understanding and analysis of the relationship between prime minister and cabinet
- Knowledge and understanding of why individuals are appointed as ministers and why individuals may lose ministerial posts
- Analysis and evaluation of the concept of presidentialism in relation to the position of the British prime minister
- Knowledge and understanding of key concepts such as collective responsibility, individual ministerial responsibility, presidentialism, spatial leadership, sofa politics, and inner cabinets

Judges and civil liberties

The nature and role of the judiciary

Note that this section refers to the judiciary in England and Wales.

The nature of the senior judiciary

British courts

The High Court

The High Court is where appeals against decisions made by public bodies tend to appear first. It is also where judges may first be asked to interpret laws and define their meaning or application.

The Appeal Court

The Appeal Court is divided into criminal and civil appeal courts. These may hear appeals from the High Court where it is felt that a further look at the interpretation of the law and the constitution by more senior judges is needed.

The Supreme Court

The 12 most senior judges sit in the Supreme Court. They (usually five of them on each case, occasionally more) hear appeals from lower courts. The judgements of the Supreme Court are considered to be binding on the whole legal system. Cases which may have wide and important political significance usually end up in the Supreme Court.

European courts

In addition to the above British courts, there are two significant European Courts.

The European Court of Human Rights

The European Court of Human Rights hears appeals concerning possible infringements of human rights. Appeals to this court take place when the British courts, including the Supreme Court, have already considered the issues. The decisions of the European Court of Human Rights are based on the **European Convention on Human Rights** (ECHR). This is controlled by the **Council of Europe** (a separate body from the EU — the council has more members than the EU and is concerned mainly with culture and rights issues). The decisions of the European Court of Human Rights are not binding on the UK Parliament, but they are very authoritative.

The European Court of Justice (ECJ)

The **European Court of Justice** is part of the EU. It hears appeals concerning the meaning and application of EU law. Its decisions are binding on the British government and Parliament.

The roles of the senior judges

Judge-made law

There are three ways in which judges are involved in developing the meaning and application of laws. These are as follows:

Declaring common law

A great deal of law is unwritten but is commonly believed to exist and to be enforceable. This is known as **common law**. Some common law — referring to the prime minister's powers or the status of individual rights, for example — has political importance. Where it is not clear what the common law is, judges may make a judgement on what the common law means and how it applies. Once a senior court has declared the meaning of common law, that interpretation is binding on all other lower courts.

Interpreting statute law

Even laws drafted in government and passed by Parliament — statutes — may not be clear. In some appeals the judges will declare what they believe the **statute law** means.

Developing case law

Even if the wording of a statute is clear, it may not always be obvious how it should be applied in particular circumstances. Judgements of this kind are known as **case law** — law as applied to particular kinds of case. Once a piece of case law has been declared, it is binding on all lower courts when they consider very similar cases.

Applying the rule of law

The rule of law (see also in the section on Constitutions) is a principle that all should be treated equally under the law. Judges are charged with the responsibility of ensuring that the rule of law applies. There are two main examples:

- Courts may conduct a **judicial review** (see below) of a decision made by a public body, especially a government department or local authority.
- Appeal courts may hear claims that a decision of a lower court treated an individual unequally.

Asserting civil liberties

Individuals and groups may claim that their rights have been abused by others or by a public body. The courts will normally consider three possible 'proofs' that this has occurred:

1 The first consideration will be whether the ECHR has been breached. This may entail interpreting the convention and deciding how it has been applied in the case they are considering.

2 The courts will then examine UK statute law to see whether there has been a breach.

3 Third, they may consider whether the case is covered by (unwritten) common law. Here the courts must decide whether there is any relevant common law and, if there is, how it applies to the particular case.

Controlling abuses of power by government

Sometimes a citizen, a group of citizens or an association of some kind may claim to have suffered because government has exceeded or abused its power. This may also be the subject of judicial review. The courts may apply a number of considerations:

- *Ultra vires* — has a public body acted within its legal powers?
- Where the action is taken by the prime minister under his or her prerogative powers, there may be a claim that the PM has exceeded those powers. Again, if the court decides the prime minister has exceeded his or her power, it can declare the action *ultra vires*.
- A senior court may decide that an action by a public body is unjust or unfair and that the public body has therefore abused its power against a citizen. In this case the court may recommend a reversal of the initial decision.

The role of European Courts

Two courts are relevant here:

The European Court of Human Rights

The European Court of Human Rights sits in Strasbourg (France) and hears appeals from citizens from all parts of Europe. It bases its decisions on the ECHR, to which most European countries are signatories. Note that this court is not part of the EU.

The European Court of Justice (ECJ)

Based in Luxembourg, the European Court of Justice is the highest court of the EU legal system. It has a number of roles:

- It settles legal disputes between EU member states.
- It settles disputes between the European Commission and a member state.
- It interprets the meaning of EU law and decides how it should be applied in specific cases and to individual countries.
- It hears appeals from individuals and groups who feel that their economic or social rights under EU law may have been abused within their own country.

The judgements of the European Court of Justice are binding on all EU member states, including the UK.

Civil liberties Rights and freedoms that are guaranteed by law, either statute law or common law. Typical examples are the rights to vote, to stand for election and to form political parties, the rights to freedom of expression, association and movement, and the rights to life and privacy.

Knowledge check 19

Distinguish between the role of the European Court of Human Rights and the European Court of Justice.

Key European cases

Table 14 gives details of some important recent cases heard in the European Court of Human Rights and the European Court of Justice.

Table 14 Key European cases

European Court of Human Rights	Detail
Votes for prisoners, 2005	The court ruled that the UK's denial of prisoners' right to vote was an abuse of their rights. In 2011, Parliament voted to ignore this ruling
DNA retention, 2008	The court ruled that it was against the ECHR right to privacy to retain the DNA profile of persons who have not been convicted of a crime. The UK government was forced to destroy many DNA profiles
Stop and search powers, 2010	The court ruled that it was an abuse of rights for the police to stop and search without any cause those attending demonstrations. These powers are now under review
European Court of Justice	**Detail**
Factortame, 1991	This case resulted in a landmark ruling that stated that the laws of the UK (in this case the Merchant Shipping Act) could not conflict with EU law (in this case the Common Fisheries Policy). This ruling transferred much sovereignty to EU law
Jobseekers' allowances, 2004	The court ruled that citizens of an EU state could claim jobseekers' allowance in the UK
Retirement age in the UK, 2009	The court ruled in favour of the UK's right to introduce a compulsory retirement age at 65
Car insurance, 2011	The court ruled that it was against EU law for car insurance companies to charge a different premium to men and women. Insurance companies have since had to change their charges

Examiner tip

Always be able to quote three or more key cases when discussing the role of courts and judges.

Judicial review

A **judicial review** is held in response to a request by an individual or association that wishes to challenge a decision or a policy adopted by a public body or a law passed by Parliament. One of the senior courts reviews the decision on one of the following grounds:

- that it offends the ECHR, i.e. is an abuse of civil liberties
- that it offends a principal of common law
- that it was *ultra vires,* that the body that made the decision did not have the legal power to do so. In other words, it was exceeding its legal powers
- that it offended natural justice and/or the rule of law. This means that the individual or association did not receive equal treatment
- that the correct administrative procedures were not followed in making a decision, for example there was insufficient consultation
- that the judgements of the courts in a judicial review are normally accepted as binding by government. However, if it is ruled that a piece of parliamentary

legislation offends common law or the ECHR, the judgement may be ignored as Parliament remains sovereign

Knowledge check 20

Why is judicial review so important?

Key examples of judicial review

Table 15 outlines four significant recent examples of judicial review.

Table 15 Examples of judicial review

Case	Effect
Mental Health Act case, 2002	The High Court ruled on the UK law that required that persons detained for mental health reasons had to prove their fitness for release. This offended the ECHR and so in future the authorities would have to prove that a person was *not* fit to be released. Asserted the human rights of those detained with mental illness
Belmarsh case, 2004	The House of Lords ruled that persons detained as suspected terrorists could not be detained without trial. A European Court of Human Rights case. The ruling was a serious blow to the government's anti-terrorism policy
Office of Fair Trading v *Abbey National* (now Santander) *and others* (2009)	An *ultra vires* case. The Supreme Court ruled that the Office of Fair Trading had no legal power to investigate bank charging practices
Suspected terrorist bank assets case, 2010	The Supreme Court ruled that the government did not have the legal power to freeze the bank assets of suspected terrorists. An *ultra vires* case. The government later passed parliamentary legislation to allow it to freeze such assets

The independence of the judiciary

Why an independent judiciary is important

An independent judiciary is important for these reasons:

- The rights of groups and individuals can be protected from abuse from government or other organisations.
- It upholds the idea that the government should not be allowed to exceed its legal powers.
- The rule of law can be better protected by independent judges.
- When there is a need to interpret the meaning and operation of the constitution, it ensures that the government is not able to manipulate the interpretation to suit itself.
- The judiciary should not be unduly influenced by any body or organisation in case it is required to dispense justice involving such a body.
- When there is a widespread public demand for a certain draconian action to be taken, for example discrimination against an ethnic minority, the violent suppression of dissident organisations or the torture of suspected terrorists, an independent judiciary can stand above public opinion and protect rights, equality and the rule of law.

Judicial independence
The principle that judges should be free from any political interference and should not be placed under political pressure when making judgements, interpretations and decisions.

How the independence of the judiciary in England and Wales is protected

- Judges cannot be dismissed on the basis of their decisions (though they can be dismissed for misconduct such as bribery). This means the government cannot put pressure on judges by threatening them with dismissal. This is often described as **security of tenure**.
- The salaries of judges are protected and guaranteed. Again this prevents the government threatening a judge with loss of income if he or she will not cooperate.
- When a case is *sub judice*, meaning that it is under way in the courts, no one, including the government and Parliament, is allowed to comment on it. This reduces political pressure on judges.
- All judges are appointed by an independent **Judicial Appointments Commission**. This means that there is little or no political interference in appointments. In this way judges do not owe any loyalty to politicians and can act independently.
- Senior judges are forbidden from engaging in active politics, so they have no party allegiances. Furthermore, as lifelong professional lawyers, they are used to putting aside their personal views when making judgements.

Evaluation of judicial independence

In evaluating judicial independence, you are considering how independent the judiciary can be in practice, despite the safeguards described above. Table 16 provides a summary.

Table 16 Judicial independence evaluated

Independence guarantees	Problems with independence
Security of tenure	Parliament remains sovereign and so ultimately controls law
Guaranteed income	
Sub judice rule	There is no entrenched constitution, so there are no clear limits to government power
Independent appointments system	
Separation of judges from politics	There is an increasing tendency for government ministers to comment adversely on judicial decisions

You should also be aware that the reform of the judiciary which was introduced in 2005 created even more independence. Three key measures were:

- The Supreme Court was created, taking the most senior judges out of the House of Lords so that they were no longer involved in politics at all.
- The Lord Chancellor used to be head of the judiciary and was a political figure, a member of the cabinet. The new head of the judiciary — the Lord Chief Justice — is not a political figure.
- The new Judicial Appointments Commission removed the last remnants of real political control over senior appointments.

Knowledge check 21

Why is the Supreme Court so important?

Judicial neutrality

The term 'judicial neutrality' refers to certain requirements and conditions made of judges which are intended to ensure that their decisions are free from bias and prejudice. The main principles are as follows:

- Judges must not be politically active, must not be active members of a political party and must not make any political statements.

- It is expected that judges should show no favour to any group in society, for example based on gender or ethnicity.

- As professional lawyers, judges are trained to make decisions based purely on law and on the rule of law, not on the basis of their personal opinions.

The nature of civil liberties

There are three related terms in the field of civil liberties, all of which require explanation. Table 17 defines the terms, indicates the associated threats and shows how each is protected:

Table 17 Civil liberties, civil rights and human rights

Term	Meaning	Examples	Threats	Forms of protection
Civil liberties	The rights of citizens that are guaranteed by law	Freedom of expression Right to privacy Freedom of association Freedom of belief	Powerful laws of libel threaten free speech Overprotection of religions threatens free speech Excessive police powers over public demonstrations Surveillance cameras	The constitutional principle of the rule of law The ECHR Common law Statutes
Civil rights	The rights of citizens in their relationship to the state	The right to vote The right to stand for election to public office The right to express political beliefs Equal and effective access to justice	Some groups, e.g. prisoners and 16-year-olds, claim they should be allowed to vote Excessive expense may deny access to justice for many	The ECHR Statute law Legal aid subsidises some in the courts The right to free legal representation for those accused of crimes Rules governing the right to a fair trial

Knowledge check 22

Why is judicial neutrality so important?

Judicial neutrality
The principle that judges should show no political or cultural bias when reaching verdicts, making decisions and deciding on interpretations. It implies that there should be a reasonably representative mixture of members of the judiciary.

Term	Meaning	Examples	Threats	Forms of protection
Human rights	Broader than civil rights, this includes the rights to equality, a decent standard of living including health, education and housing	Sex equality Equal opportunities for all Rights to welfare	Sex discrimination Racial discrimination Age and disability discrimination Variations in the quality of health and education provision	The principles of the United Nations Anti-discrimination legislation Judicial reviews asserting the rule of law EU law The ECHR

Examiner tip

Make sure you can distinguish between judicial neutrality and judicial independence. Students often confuse the two.

The Human Rights Act

Its operation

The Human Rights Act was passed in 1998 and came into force in 2000. Its effect was to bring the terms of the **European Convention on Human Rights** (ECHR) into British law. The following arrangements were made under the Act.

- All government bodies, state organisations, devolved assemblies and governments, local authorities and any body engaged in 'public business' such as schools, hospitals or the media, must abide by the terms of the convention.
- The only body that is not bound by the ECHR is the UK Parliament in Westminster. This means that parliamentary sovereignty is preserved.
- If legislation proposed in Westminster is likely to contradict the convention, the relevant government minister must make a 'declaration of incompatibility', stating how and why the proposal does not conform to the convention.
- Any legal claim that the convention has been breached can be made in a British court at any level. If the judge believes the convention has been breached, he or she can order that a decision or action must be changed or cancelled.
- Appeals based on the convention can be passed up to higher courts, ultimately to the Supreme Court.
- Judges in the courts can interpret the meaning of the ECHR and how it should apply in a particular case.
- The one limitation on the power of the judges is that they cannot overturn any law made in the UK Parliament. The judge may declare that the convention has been breached by such an Act or Order, but cannot overturn it.
- In some cases of great significance, a final appeal may be made to the European Court of Human Rights in Strasbourg.
- Judgements of the European Court of Human Rights are binding in most countries, but not in the UK. Nevertheless, the UK government will virtually always abide by its decisions.

Examiner tip

Make sure that you remember that the European Convention on Human Rights has nothing to do with the EU. It comes from the Council of Europe, a different body.

Examples of the terms of the ECHR

There is a wide range of rights asserted in the ECHR. Some examples of prominent rights are:

- the right to life
- the right to privacy and family life
- the right to free expression
- the right to free assembly
- the right to free belief
- the right to be free from discrimination of various kinds
- the right to a fair trial

Key cases under the ECHR

Table 18 describes a number of cases which have been dealt with under the ECHR.

Table 18 ECHR cases

Case	Detail
Afghan hijackers case, 2006	A controversial ruling that a group of Afghan refugees who had hijacked a plane to the UK could claim asylum and seek work in the UK on the grounds that their lives were in danger if they were deported
Mosley v News of the World (2008)	Max Mosley, a Formula 1 executive, claimed his privacy had been invaded when details of a sadomasochist party he attended was reported in the *News of the World*, with several false details. He was awarded compensation
Insurance discrimination case, 2011	The European Court of Human Rights ruled that insurance companies could not discriminate against men by charging them higher car insurance premiums than women

Knowledge check 23

Why is the Human Rights Act so important?

Judicial protection of civil liberties

How judges can protect civil liberties

This section summarises the various ways in which judges in the UK and in the European Court of Human Rights or the European Court of Justice can protect individual and group rights:

- They can refer to the ECHR and decide that a right has been infringed. They may reverse a decision and/or order compensation.
- They may declare that common law has been offended and change a decision.
- They may refer to a parliamentary statute (such as equal opportunities legislation) which protects a particular right. This will be enforced.
- They may similarly refer to a piece of EU legislation.
- A judicial review may take place on the request of a citizen.

Evaluation of judicial protection of liberties

Strengths

- The passage of the Human Rights Act has added a codified set of rights to which judges can refer.

- Particularly since the 1960s there has been a large quantity of legislation passed that asserts civil liberties, in particular laws forbidding discrimination of various kinds.
- As the judiciary has become steadily more independent, it has also become more active in its protection of rights.
- The growth of judicial review, to many thousands of cases each year today, has brought judges to the forefront of enforcing rights and equality.

Limitations

- The courts cannot be proactive in their protection of rights. This means they must wait for appeals to be launched by citizens.
- Because the ECHR is not binding on Parliament, the judges are powerless to overturn laws that infringe rights.
- When judges do assert rights through common law or the ECHR, they cannot prevent the government from passing new legislation to prevent the courts making similar decisions in the future.

Judicial power

Evaluation of judicial power over government

Table 19 summarises the main strengths and weaknesses of the power of the judiciary in relation to government.

Table 19 Evaluating judicial power

Strengths	Weaknesses
Judicial reviews have a wide scope to deal with claimed abuses of governmental power	The absence of a codified constitution and the existence of ill-defined government powers make it difficult to judge whether power has been abused
The Human Rights Act has added power to judges to prevent government from exercising excessive power which threatens rights	Parliamentary sovereignty means that a government that controls its parliamentary majority can grant powers to itself or its agencies through legislation and the judiciary can do nothing to prevent this
The conventions and statutes concerning the independence of the judiciary have resulted in a more active judiciary	Parliament can place constraints on the judiciary in its sentencing powers
Judges retain wide powers over the sentencing of convicted criminals	Government and Parliament can claim that judges are unelected and unaccountable and so do not have the right to challenge the power of the elected and accountable government and Parliament

Key cases in judicial power

There are a number of recent examples of cases which have illustrated the power of the courts in relation to government (all 2010):

- ***Child Poverty Action Group* v *Secretary of State for Work and Pensions*** An important ruling that the Department of Work and Pensions did not have the legal power to force people to return overpayments of welfare benefits when the department was at fault. An *ultra vires* case.

Knowledge check 24

Why is it significant that judges are neither elected nor politically accountable for their decisions?

Examiner tip

Make sure you know at least three cases to illustrate the power of the judiciary over government.

- *Family of Justin Smith* v *Secretary of State for Defence* The Supreme Court ruled that the ECHR does *not* normally have any force with troops serving abroad.
- *HM Treasury* v *Mohammed Jabar Ahmed* The Supreme Court ruled that the government did *not* have the power to freeze the financial assets of suspected terrorists.

As we can see from the above cases, the Supreme Court rules both in favour of and against the government, judging its cases purely on its interpretation of existing law.

Reform of the judiciary

The main recent reforms of the judiciary are contained in the **Constitutional Reform Act** of 2005. Its main provisions were as follows:

- The Lord Chancellor — who had been head of the legal system, a cabinet minister and speaker of the House of Lords — was to lose most of his roles in terms of running the judicial system and return to a largely ceremonial position.
- The Lord Chief Justice (a non-political judge) was to be put in charge of the legal system.
- A new political post of Secretary of State for Justice was to be created. The holder sits in cabinet, but is forbidden from interfering with court decisions.
- A new Supreme Court was to be set up (it began operation in 2009). This has the same powers as the judicial committee of the House of Lords (known as the 'Law Lords'), which it replaced. It is the highest appeal court in the UK and is now separate from the House of Lords. New members of the court will not necessarily be granted a peerage.
- Appointments to the Supreme Court were to be made by a senior judicial committee which was to be free from political interference.
- Appointments to the judiciary in general were to be put in the hands of an independent Judicial Appointments Commission. Again, this is free from political interference although the prime minister can veto a controversial appointment.

Judges and civil liberties

- The nature of individual rights and liberties, why they are threatened and how they can be protected
- Knowledge and understanding of the ways in which the judiciary specifically can protect rights and liberties
- Analysis and evaluation of how far judges can protect rights and liberties
- Knowledge and understanding of the role of the judiciary in interpreting and developing law
- Critical evaluation of the political role of the judiciary

- Knowledge and understanding of the relationships between the judiciary, government and Parliament
- Analysis and evaluation of how far the judiciary can control the power of government
- Knowledge, understanding and evaluation of the extent to which senior judges are independent and neutral
- Knowledge and understanding of reforms of the judiciary since 2005
- Knowledge and understanding of the relationships between European and UK courts
- Knowledge and understanding of key concepts relating to the judiciary

Knowledge summary

Questions & Answers

How to use this section

At the beginning of this section there is a guide to the structure of the examination for Unit 2, followed by an explanation of the assessment objectives and a guide as to how the marks for each assessment objective are distributed among the different questions on the paper. It is important that you familiarise yourself with all three of these features — the exam structure, the nature of assessment objectives and how you can score marks for each of those assessment objectives.

There follow some specimen examination questions. These are neither past examination questions, nor future examination questions, but they are very similar to the kinds of questions you will face.

The best way to use this section of the guide is to look at each question and make notes on how you would go about answering it, including the key facts and knowledge you would use, relevant examples, the analysis, arguments and evaluations you would deploy and the conclusions you would reach. You should also make a plan of how you would answer the whole question, taking into account the examiner tip (indicated by the icon ⓔ) immediately below the question.

After each specimen question there are two exemplar answers. One will be a strong answer and the other will be either weak or of medium quality. The strength of each specimen answer is indicated in the examiner commentary (again indicated by the icon ⓔ) that follows it. In the commentary there are also notes on the answer's strengths and weaknesses and an indication as to how marks would be awarded for each assessment objective. Now compare these specimen answers with your own notes. Amend your notes to bring them to the standard of the stronger specimen. Having done all this, you can now attempt a full answer to the question, aiming to avoid the weaknesses and include the strengths that have been indicated in the specimen answers and explanations of the marks.

Of course you may use the information in your own way. The above guidance is merely a recommendation. Remember, however, that simply 'learning' the strong specimen answers will not help — they are answers to specimen questions, not to the questions you will actually face. It is preferable to learn how to answer questions 'actively', that is by writing your own answers, using the questions and answers as a guide. In this way you will be able to tackle effectively any questions that may come your way in the examination.

The structure of the examination

The examination is divided into two sections — A and B. Each of these two sections contains two questions. You are required to select *one* question from each section and answer *all* parts of that question. Of the total of four questions on the paper, each will concern one of the four sections of the specification. In other words, all four specification topics will appear on the paper. Individual questions will not, however, require specific knowledge beyond what is included in the specification section (though candidates may bring in relevant knowledge to their answers from any part of the specification). One hour and 20 minutes is allowed for the examination and students are advised to divide their time equally between sections A and B, i.e. 40 minutes each. Each section carries up to 40 marks. *It is therefore a general principle that students are expected to spend about 1 minute of their time for each mark available.* So, for a 5-mark question, use 5 minutes, for a 10-mark question, use 10 minutes and so on.

Section A

Section A contains two stimulus–response questions. The questions may be from any of the four sections of the Unit 2 specification. The stimulus material (or source) may be in the form of a commentary, a newspaper article, extracts from a book or even a well-known blog. It may also be in the form of some statistics, for example the make-up of the membership of the House of Lords in figures. There may occasionally be two pieces of stimulus material for one question.

The question will be divided into three parts — (a), (b) and (c).

Part (a) scores up to 5 marks and is a straightforward exercise in identifying facts and issues (normally only two) from the source and offering a brief explanation of each of them. You are expected to spend about 5 minutes on part (a) questions.

Part (b) scores up to 10 marks and is an exercise in identifying facts and issues from the stimulus material, but also adding information and/or analysis from one's own knowledge. One's own knowledge may be used to include additional facts or issues and/or may be used to offer explanations and analysis not included in the stimulus material.

Part (c) scores up to 25 marks. The stimulus material is not needed to answer this question, though it will be on the same topic area as the first two parts. Of course, candidates may use information from the stimulus in their answers, if appropriate. Answers to part (c) questions take the form of a short essay.

Section B

Section B has a simpler structure. It consists of two essay-style questions, from which candidates must choose one. The questions are worth 40 marks each and so it is expected that students will spend approximately 40 minutes on their Section B answer.

A typical examination might, therefore, look like this:

Section A

Answer *one* question from Section A

Question 1: stimulus-based question on the constitution
(a) 5-mark question
(b) 10-mark question
(c) 25-mark question

Question 2: stimulus-based question on the judiciary
(a) 5-mark question
(b) 10-mark question
(c) 25-mark question

Total marks for Section A = 40

Section B

Answer *one* question from Section B

Question 3: essay-style question on the prime minister and cabinet (40 marks)

Question 4: essay-style question on Parliament (40 marks)

Total marks for Section B = 40

Total marks for the examination = 80

The nature of assessment objectives

There are three assessment objectives, described in the table below. Assessment objectives have two purposes. First, they are a guide for students, demonstrating the kind of knowledge, understanding and skills they need to do well in the examination. Second, they are a guide to those who will mark the examination. Markers do not merely give marks for their overall impression of an answer. Instead they mark 'by assessment objective'. This means that they may award marks for up to three separate assessment objectives. Thus a candidate may do well on assessment objectives 1 and 2 but poorly on 3, or well on all three, or poorly on them all. Markers must 'dissect' an answer to decide how well a candidate has been able to meet each of the assessment objectives.

These are the descriptions of the three assessment objectives published by Edexcel, who set and organise the marking of this Unit:

Assessment objective	Skills required
AO1	Demonstrate knowledge and understanding of relevant institutions, processes, political concepts, theories and debates
AO2	Analyse and evaluate political information, arguments and explanations, and identify parallels, connections, similarities and differences between the aspects of the political systems studied
AO3	Construct and communicate coherent arguments making use of a range of appropriate political vocabulary

To give an idea of what these mean in practice, we may consider a topic and look at typical knowledge and skills required:

Questions on constitutional reform

AO1
- What constitutional reforms have been introduced since 1997?
- Why were they introduced?
- What were the impacts of these reforms?
- What reforms were incomplete or promised but not yet delivered?
- What reforms are currently proposed?
- For what reasons are these reforms proposed?

AO2
- To what extent have the reforms been successful?
- To what extent have they had an impact?
- What were the specifically political reasons for introducing them?
- Why have they been supported or opposed?
- Why did they have the effects they have had?

AO3
- Use of appropriate political vocabulary such as codification, entrenchment, democratisation, decentralisation, modernisation, rights culture, devolution
- Structure of the answer, including a logical introduction, clearly explained content and a cogent conclusion, supported by evidence

We can further explain the use of assessment objectives by adding the following:

AO1 involves the knowledge of facts, key recent historical developments, how institutions work, how institutions are connected and interact, how institutions have changed and evolved, examples to illustrate theories, explanations of the main arguments for and against an issue.

AO2 involves explaining *why* certain developments have taken place, linkages between cause and effect, evaluations such as 'to what extent?' or 'how much?', analysis of the relationships between political opinion and political changes, explanations and explorations of the relationships between institutions.

AO3 means clarity of meaning, use of vocabulary and structure of answer. Spelling and handwriting are of relatively minor importance as long as poor spelling or handwriting does not make meanings unclear.

The distribution of assessment objectives

Different questions and parts of questions each carry a different distribution of assessment objective marks. It is important to be familiar with these as it should affect the way you answer a particular question. The distribution is as follows (using the same exemplar exam structure shown above):

Section A

Question 1: stimulus-based question on the constitution

(a) 5-mark question: all 5 marks for AO1

(b) 10-mark question: 7 marks for AO1, 3 marks for AO2

(c) 25-mark question: 8 marks for AO1, 9 marks for AO2, 8 marks for AO3

Question 2: stimulus-based question on the judiciary

(a) 5-mark question: all 5 marks for AO1

(b) 10-mark question: 7 marks for AO1, 3 marks for AO2

(c) 25-mark question: 8 marks for AO1, 9 marks for AO2, 8 marks for AO3

Total marks for Section A = 40 (20 marks for AO1, 12 marks for AO2, 8 marks for AO3)

Section B

Question 3: essay-style question on the prime minister and cabinet (40 marks): **20 marks for AO1, 12 marks for AO2, 8 marks for AO3**

Question 4: essay-style question on Parliament (40 marks): **20 marks for AO1, 12 marks for AO2, 8 marks for AO3**

Total marks for Section B = 40 (20 marks for AO1, 12 marks for AO2, 8 marks for AO3)

Total marks for the examination = 80
(40 marks for AO1, 24 marks for AO2, 16 marks for AO3)

We can identify a number of key points from the scheme of assessment:

Questions 1(a) and 2(a) involve *only* marks under AO1 (knowledge and understanding), so no analysis or evaluation is required. The structure of the answer is also immaterial as long as the meanings are clear.

Questions 1(b) and 2(b) involve *mostly* marks under AO1, but some analysis is required, albeit limited.

Marks for questions 1(c) and 2(c) are evenly distributed across all three assessment objectives, so a well-rounded, well-structured answer is needed.

Questions 3 and 4 are weighted towards AO1, so there is a need for a large volume of facts, information, understanding and examples. Nevertheless AO2 and AO3 remain relatively important.

The constitution

Question 1 Stimulus-based question

Read the following passage and answer the questions that follow.

The coalition government that took office in May 2010 was determined to make some effective reforms to the British Constitution. This was a difficult task given that the Liberal Democrats are, by nature, a reformist party, whereas, as their name suggests, Conservatives are reluctant to support radical change. But David Cameron was personally determined to modernise the constitution, without threatening any major political upheaval. Thus Cameron and most Conservatives declared that they were opposed to a change in the electoral system, but did recognise the need to complete the reform of the House of Lords. These two measures were part of the price of reaching agreement with Nick Clegg and the Liberal Democrats in the coalition negotiations. The idea of introducing fixed-term parliaments — with elections every 5 years — was something of a surprise. But one could understand how it came about. Liberal Democrats have long supported the move, while the Conservatives hope to create stability by guaranteeing the life of the coalition until 2015. Cameron's determination to have electoral boundaries redrawn so that each constituency would be equal was also understandable as it would remove Labour's inbuilt advantage as a result of the way the constituencies are currently unevenly sized.

(a) With reference to the source, explain any two constitutional reforms proposed by the coalition.

(5 marks)

🅮 With short part (a) questions, always include a little explanation. Avoid quoting word for word from the stimulus text.

Student A

From the source, two constitutional reforms are: first a change in the electoral system. The favoured choice was the alternative vote system. Its introduction was made subject to a referendum. The second was to reform the House of Lords. This involved either a completely elected, or a partly elected, partly appointed House, with hereditary peers losing their voting rights.

🅮 **5/5 marks awarded.** All marks are for AO1 (knowledge and understanding) so no discussion or analysis is required. The answer accurately identifies two reforms mentioned in the source. It explains each one briefly. This is an A-grade answer.

Student B

Two reforms are electoral reform and reform of the House of Lords. These were very controversial and there were problems agreeing them in the coalition.

ⓔ **2/5 marks awarded.** The second sentence is redundant and receives no marks. It is discussing the reforms, and discussion is not required. The candidate receives 2 marks for correctly identifying two reforms, but no more as they are not explained. This answer would achieve a D grade.

(b) With reference to the source and your own knowledge, explain why the coalition government embarked on a programme of constitutional reform. (10 marks)

ⓔ Try to include as much of your own knowledge as possible. Do this by including additional points not mentioned in the source, and some analysis which comes from your own knowledge. This does not have to be enormously sophisticated, but it should go beyond the material in the source.

Student A

From the source we can identify a number of reasons for these proposed reforms. The first was the influence of David Cameron who wanted to modernise the constitution. Cameron came to office wanting to appear as a modern prime minister with some liberal ideas and not just a typical traditional Tory. The second reason concerns electoral reform. The Liberal Democrats have always wanted a 'fairer' electoral system and so they were bound to demand reform as a price for entering the coalition. Even though AV is a compromise reform, they agreed to it, perhaps believing it was the best they would get as the Tories would not stomach PR. Third, fixed-term parliaments were a way of, hopefully, guaranteeing the survival of the coalition. Coalitions tend to be weak and fragile, so the fixed term would help it last until 2015.

In addition, there is a general consensus that the House of Lords needs to be reformed and the coalition wanted to finish the job which had been abandoned by New Labour. The Lords is an outdated institution and both parties in the coalition wanted to be modern. Making constituency sizes more equal is controversial because it is said that it reduces the disadvantage the Conservatives have in elections. This gives a clear reason why Cameron was so determined to make this reform. He also wants to reduce the overall size of the House of Commons. This is a cost-saving measure.

ⓔ **8/10 marks awarded:** 6/7 for AO1 and 2/3 for AO2. A number of positive features can be identified in the answer. First, the student has used material from the stimulus text and added a good deal of own knowledge, clearly stating what is from the passage and what is additional — this is a good practice. Second, the student has expanded on the information in the passage, briefly analysing Cameron's 'modernism' and looking at some of the dynamics of the coalition agreement. The marks for AO1 are achieved because of the good knowledge and understanding of five reforms, while AO2 marks are achieved by engaging in some analysis of the reasons for the reforms. Another mark or two could have been gained under AO1 if there had been reference made to the disrepute into which Parliament had fallen so some reforms could be seen as an answer to public concerns. Similarly, another AO2 mark would have been awarded had the final two points been more fully developed. This answer would gain an A grade.

Student B

The coalition government decided to make three main reforms. These were as follows. The first reform was to introduce AV after a referendum. This was because the Liberal Democrats insisted on such a reform — otherwise they wouldn't have joined with the Conservatives. The Conservatives don't want AV or any reforms but they had to agree to the referendum or they would not have been in government with the Lib Dems. Another reform was the introduction of fixed-term parliaments so that both parties knew that the coalition would last for at least 5 years. The third reform was the change in the House of Lords to an elected second chamber. This also had to be done because it was a Lib Dem demand. It also made Cameron appear to be a really modern prime minister. But we could say that Cameron really only accepted the reforms because he had to appease the more radical Liberal Democrats.

@ **5/10 marks awarded:** 3/7 for AO1 and 2/3 for AO2. This response is at the bottom of the C-grade band. The main reason why this is only a medium quality answer is that it demonstrates too little of the student's own knowledge. It scarcely goes beyond the passage either in terms of content (only three reforms mentioned) or in terms of analysis. It does achieve some marks under AO1 because the reasons for the three main reforms are identified and briefly explained. However, the marks for AO2 are limited because there is no analysis beyond what can be found in the passage itself. So, for example, the student should have expanded specifically on the nature of the coalition agreement — the Lib Dems were bound to demand reforms as the price of their cooperation as such reforms are a central part of their policy. A further reason for reform was that Parliament had fallen into disrepute and so Cameron was determined to reform it. This particularly applies to the proposal to allow constituencies to 'recall' unsatisfactory MPs — a direct response to the expenses scandal. This is not mentioned in the source and so would be credited as additional knowledge.

(c) To what extent can the British Constitution be seen as 'outdated'? (25 marks)

@ Aim to give a balanced answer, presenting arguments on both sides of a case. It is also important, even for 25-mark questions, to have a structure, with a clear introduction and conclusion. A tip about conclusions: if you are stuck for what to say, pick out one or two arguments which are stronger than the others and so might swing the conclusion one way or another.

Student A

This essay will first examine what is meant by the term 'outdated' and then will go on to consider the aspects of the constitution that are outdated and those which are not. Finally I will consider whether it is so outdated that it needs seriously reforming to make it more modern. **a**

The first meaning of outdated is that it no longer conforms to a modern democracy. In the modern world we expect that government will be controlled and that human rights will be firmly protected. We also expect that there should be a great deal of democratic influence from the people and pressure groups. The second meaning is that it is not like other modern constitutions in the world. Britain prides itself on being 'different', but this should give way to appearing modern and up to date. We still have old-fashioned, undemocratic institutions. A third meaning of 'outdated' would be that it is too centralised when modern political systems are expected to take into account the aspirations of local people and national regions. **b**

The British constitution is certainly out of date in that it is not codified. Virtually all constitutions are codified these days. It may have been satisfactory at one time, but we now need a codified constitution so that there is a proper separation of powers, better protection of human rights and so that people can understand and relate to it. It is also out of date because we operate an electoral system which is designed to preserve the two-party system and keeps out smaller parties that represent different groups in society. Excessive executive power is another problem because it denies the will of the people and Parliament. There is a new spirit of democratic renewal in the world and Britain is not responding.

We are also outdated in that we persist with undemocratic institutions. We still do not have an elected second chamber and many of the powers of the prime minister depend upon the unelected, hereditary monarchy. **c**

At the same time there are some aspects that are not out of date. Devolution has been introduced with proportional electoral systems. The Human Rights Act and the Freedom of Information Act have gone a long way to protecting individual liberties and to improving public awareness of issues. We also have modernised the judiciary by introducing the Supreme Court and making sure of an independent judiciary. We also have more referendums nowadays so that there is more popular democracy than ever before.

But in the end, and in conclusion, we have to say that the British Constitution is still outdated. It is true that it has been greatly modernised since 1997 and that modernisation is still happening, but it is out of date for two main reasons. First that it is not codified, which means it can be easily interfered with by powerful governments and rights are not fully protected. Secondly, Parliament, especially the Lords, is too weak and not modern enough to deal with modern popular democracy and proper accountability of government. **d**

e **22/25 marks awarded:** 6/8 for AO1, 8/9 for AO2 and 8/8 for AO3. This is an A-grade answer, scoring well on all three assessment objectives. It has wide knowledge and understanding of the issues, of the ways in which the constitution has or has not been brought more up to date, and is aware of the meaning of the term 'outdated'. There is a clear structure and the content is clearly explained. However, a couple of AO1 marks are missing as there are a couple of key points omitted (for example, the lack of separation of powers and prerogative powers). On AO2 the answer undertakes a full evaluation, looking at both sides of the issue. It also analyses what is meant by 'outdated' and is able to distinguish between aspects which could be said to be outdated and those which are modern. It would receive a top AO3 mark.

a An excellent introduction addresses the question and gives guidance as to how the student is going to answer it. **b** The second paragraph is an excellent passage in that it considers what 'outdated' means. This is called 'deconstructing' the question and is very good practice). **c** The one major weakness of this answer is that some key points are not fully explained. **d** A clear, firm conclusion is supported by the evidence presented, with reasons why that conclusion has been reached. Overall, there is also good use made of political vocabulary, with such words and phrases as 'democratic renewal', 'accountability', 'separation of powers', 'popular democracy' and 'codification'.

Student B

The main reason the British Constitution is outdated is that it is not codified. Virtually all constitutions in the world are codified today so Britain is well out of line with modern practices. An uncodified constitution does have advantages — it is flexible and can adapt to modern conditions, such as terrorism etc. It has also lasted for a long time so we can use the conservative idea that 'if it ain't broke, don't fix it'. **a**

It is also outdated because it has so many unelected parts. We have the monarchy and the House of Lords and far too many quangos. It is essential that all parts of the constitution should be fully elected. We also do not protect human rights enough and everywhere today rights are well protected, especially in Europe. **b**

The constitution is out of date because we do not have a proper separation of powers, as exists in the USA. Government is far too strong and Parliament is too weak. This is out date and we need to introduce more controls over strong government. For example, the Terrorism Acts were not well challenged and yet they threatened human rights a great deal.

People want to be involved more in politics today, but there is no codified constitution that they can see and identify with it. We need a modern constitution which will allow more people to participate instead of being forced to accept over-powerful government. **c**

There are some ways in which it is modern — the Human Rights Act and devolution, for example, do make it up to date, but these cannot compete with the ways I have described that make it outdated. So, in conclusion, yes the constitution is outdated and needs serious reform to make it more modern. **d**

e **13/25 marks awarded:** 3/8 for AO1, 5/9 for AO2 and 5/8 for AO3. This is a D-grade answer. Its main weakness is that it is unbalanced. It makes a reasonably good case for the argument that the British Constitution is outdated, but there is very little on the other side of the issue. It also has a weak structure, with no real introduction. Most of it is clear enough, however, so it does not score too badly on AO3, but there is little 'political' vocabulary. Finally, it loses AO1 marks because not a wide enough range of issues is covered.

a The first paragraph is not bad, but perhaps needs to range across a few more issues than just codification. **b** The second paragraph makes some good points, but more is needed on how far they have modernised the constitution. **c** Similarly in the next paragraph, where the issue needs much more development — how have reforms addressed or failed to address this problem? **d** The attempt at balance is welcome, but it needs a much fuller treatment, for example referring to the Supreme Court or devolution as examples of modernisation.

Question 2 **Essay-style question**

To what extent has the British Constitution been effectively reformed since 1997? (40 marks)

ⓔ It is important to read the question carefully. Try to respond to what the question actually says by identifying the key words — in this case they are 'to what extent?' and 'effectively'. Beware of reproducing an essay you may have done for homework which *looked* similar.

Student A

The New Labour government that took power in 1997 began to reform the British Constitution, introducing the Human Rights Act, devolution and some reform of the Lords among other less important changes. Unfortunately Labour did not complete those reforms and a great deal was left undone. The question since then is how much has the constitution been reformed and how much positive effect these reforms have had. **a**

There is no doubt that the Human Rights Act has transformed Britain. It created a means by which government and other bodies could be prevented from abusing our rights. The courts were given powers to enforce rights. This has meant that we now have more privacy and have the right to be treated equally under the law. However, the HRA was not made binding on Parliament and so governments can still abuse rights. This has been seen with the anti-terrorism acts, which give the police great powers, including the ability to introduce control orders (originally imprisonment) without trial. The HRA also does not protect us against the growth of surveillance and stop-and-search powers or the prevention of some demonstrations. Similarly, the Freedom of Information Act has been partly effective. **b** It enabled us to know about the MPs' expenses scandal and other aspects of government. However, government can still conceal sensitive information. Perhaps the FOI Act should have been stronger.

Devolution was well supported in Scotland and Wales and has made a huge difference in those countries as well as in Northern Ireland. The people of those countries support devolution and have demanded more. This is the main issue — that devolution perhaps did not go far enough. Some also suggest there should be proper federalism for these countries to have true independence. So it has been effective in decentralising government, but not effective because there is still an appetite for more independence in Scotland and Wales. However, it seems that soon more powers will be devolved to Wales and Scotland so the process is ongoing.

The reform of the House of Lords by removing all but 92 of the hereditary peers had some impact. This was effective in that it made the Lords less undemocratic, but it did not make it democratic. If we are to have a truly effective second chamber it will need to be elected and therefore accountable, many argue. The creation of the Supreme Court has helped to make the judiciary appear more independent, but the new court has no more power than the old House of Lords. Therefore it does not have more ability to effectively control government power. The judges cannot overturn what parliament legislates and so they are very limited. **c**

Some reforms were not made at all. For example, Labour promised to introduce proportional representation for general elections but it dropped this proposal when it came to power. We are still operating with an outdated electoral system that preserves the two-party system and gives too much power to government. PR was introduced in devolved governments but not at Westminster. So the plans to have more control over the two main parties have not been effective. Similarly, we have still not seen effective reform of the Lords.

Gordon Brown promised to reform the prerogative powers of the prime minister, but nothing was done and we still operate the ancient system where the prime minister has a great deal of arbitrary power from the royal prerogative. **d**

The coalition government has introduced fixed-term parliaments but it is too early to say whether this will be effective. It will stop the prime minister having the power to call an election to his own party's advantage, but it is not clear whether this will effectively control his power. **e** The other reforms — to reduce the size of the Commons and equalise the size of constituencies — do not seem to be significant, so effectiveness cannot be judged.

Some say that the most effective reform would be to codify and entrench the constitution. They argue that this will help to control too much executive power, will help to effectively protect human rights and will be clearer for people to understand. **f** On the other hand, such a constitutional change may not be effective because it might make it less flexible and unable to adapt to changing circumstances (such as the recent hung parliament and coalition government).

So we must conclude that there is a mixed picture. Today, compared to 1997, Britain is more democratic and human rights are much better protected. The people are entitled to more information and in Scotland, Wales and Northern Ireland government is more sensitive to public opinion. On the other hand, there is still much to be done in the fields of electoral reform and changes to the House of Lords. We can therefore say the constitution has only been partly effectively reformed, but steps are being taken to make it more effective in the future. But until it is codified and entrenched it will always be vulnerable to the actions of powerful governments. **g**

ⓔ 29/40 marks awarded: 16/20 for AO1, 7/12 for AO2 and 29/40 for AO3. This is a strong A-grade answer in that it is very focused on the question. **a b** It identifies 'effectively' as a key term and constantly refers to the idea of effectiveness, sometimes addressing the question directly. It is also reasonably comprehensive in that it deals with more of the reforms that have taken place since 1997. It does have two weaknesses. One is that its analyses of the effectiveness of the reforms are not well developed. **c** For example, specific examples of effectiveness could have been added — important examples of House of Lords action or key court cases; and **d** in paragraph 6 possibly a little more development, perhaps criticising arbitrary power. The points made are valid but lack depth. Second, the answer is not very sophisticated in its use of political vocabulary. It therefore scores much better on AO1 than on AO2 and AO3. Fortunately the distribution of assessment objectives is biased towards AO1 in Section B of the exam.

e f There are some excellent examples of clever, concise evaluation. **g** The conclusion is good, though slightly ambivalent. It could be more decisive, but this is not a problem. It does reflect the evidence presented and it does provide a specific answer — that reform has been partially effective. Another strength is the introduction. It sets the scene effectively and then deconstructs the question.

Student B

There has been a great deal of reform of the constitution since 1997. The following reforms have been made: the introduction of the Human Rights Act, reform of the Lords, devolution of power to Scotland and Wales, the creation of the Supreme Court and the introduction of fixed-term parliaments. However, some of these reforms are incomplete and others have not been made at all. This essay will examine the extent to which reforms have been made and will look at the reforms which have been supported but have not been introduced. Finally, I will consider whether the constitution has been effectively reformed. **a**

It is said that devolution is a process and not an event so there is quite a bit to go before it is complete. For example, the Welsh Assembly cannot make laws and none of the devolved governments can collect their own taxes, though Scotland can vary income tax by 3%. Until Scotland and Wales control their own economies the devolution process will not be complete.

The Human Rights Act brings the European Convention on Human Rights into UK law. But this is something of an illusion because Parliament does not have to abide by the Act as long as a declaration of incompatibility is made. Unless the HRA is properly entrenched it is an incomplete reform. **b**

The House of Lords is a very incomplete reform. It remains an unelected, unaccountable chamber even though most of the hereditary peers have been removed. It looks as though the coalition is going to complete the reform, but at the moment it is far from complete.

One reform that looks to be completed, however, is the creation of the Supreme Court and the removal of the Lord Chancellor, a cabinet minister, from being head of the judiciary and speaker of the House of Lords. This creates a more independent judiciary.

There are two reforms that have not been done at all. One is electoral reform and the other is the codifying of the constitution. Labour promised to introduce PR at elections in 1997 but lost interest in it and it was never implemented. Despite proposals to introduce AV we still have an unfair electoral system — FPTP in the UK. Nor has the constitution been codified, although many politicians, especially liberals, have argued that it should be to bring Britain in line with the rest of the world. **c**

The coalition is also tinkering with the constitution and there is much talk of a British Bill of Rights, but as yet the only change is the introduction of fixed-term parliaments so the prime minister can no longer choose the general election date.

So constitutional reform in Britain is still a 'work in progress'. The really big issues of electoral reform, an elected House of Lords and a codified constitution have all been fudged. Our flexible, uncodified constitution is still in need of a great deal of reform. **d**

ⓔ **22/40 marks awarded:** 12/20 for AO1, 5/12 for AO2 and 5/8 for AO3. As it stands, this answer scores a C grade. It would have received a higher grade had the question been slightly different. If the word 'effectively' were absent from the question, the answer would have addressed the question adequately. But this answer simply ignores whether the reforms which have taken place have been effective. **a** For example, in an otherwise well-conceived introduction, 'effectiveness' is not addressed. The answer is merely an evaluation of how much reform there has been and what is still left to be done. **d** The conclusion too does not really address the question.

This illustrates the importance of *addressing every part of the question* and not simply reproducing the answer the candidate hoped for. The answer scores quite well on AO1, but loses many of the AO2 marks because it fails to evaluate the effectiveness of the reforms. **b** Paragraph 3 offers a good point but not nearly enough evaluation of the HRA, which is a key reform, and **c** in paragraph 6 more evaluation and analysis is needed on codification — what might it achieve? The AO1 marks will not compensate for the lack of accurate focus. Fortunately, the answer is clearly written, though rather unsophisticated, and does quite well on AO3 marks.

Parliament

Question 3 **Stimulus-based question**

Study the following data and answer the questions which follow:

Political make-up of Parliament, 2010

House of Commons		House of Lords	
Conservative	305	Labour	242
Labour	255	Conservative	219
Lib Dem	57	Crossbenchers	183
Green	1	Lib Dem	94
Others	32	Bishops	26
Total	650		

(a) From the source, identify three ways in which the political make-up of the House of Lords differs from that of the Commons.

(5 marks)

ⓔ There are some important lessons in this little question. First it is always important to distinguish between an 'absolute majority' — when a party has more than 50% of the votes or seats — and a 'plurality', when a party has more seats or votes than another but is short of an absolute majority of 50%+. Second, every word in the question may be significant. Here the word 'political' is vital. It requires the answer to refer to parties and party allegiances. Third, if the question asks for two or three responses (three in this case), there is no harm in doing more, though you may waste valuable time by doing so.

Student A

First, it is clear that a different party has the largest group. In the Commons the Conservatives are the largest party, but in the Lords, Labour is the biggest. Second, there are a large number of crossbenchers (neutral peers) in the Lords, but all members of the Commons belong to a party. Third, there are 26 Bishops in the Lords, not in the Commons. Fourth, there is one Green MP but none in the Lords as far as we know.

ⓔ **5/5 marks awarded:** All marks are for AO1. This A-grade response gives four differences, which is not necessary but does no harm. All the differences are accurately described. The student has found several differences and explained each one simply but clearly.

Student B

> The Conservatives have a majority in the Commons but not in the Lords. There are also many crossbenchers in the Lords but not in the House of Commons. There are bishops in the Lords but not in Commons.

ⓔ **2/5 marks awarded:** all for AO1. The first aspect of the answer is wrong as the Conservatives do not have a majority in either House. They are the *biggest* party in the Commons, but they do not have a majority. The comment on crossbenchers is correct but the student should have stated (as the A-grade answer does) that they are neutral, as the question refers to the 'political' make-up of Parliament. The observation about the bishops is true, but is not a political point as the question asks. So three points are made but none is fully correct — a D-grade answer.

(b) From the source and your own knowledge, how representative is Parliament?   (10 marks)

ⓔ It is advisable with part (b) questions to try to balance information from the source with 'own knowledge'. Own knowledge can be additional analysis or additional facts and information. When searching for additional information and analysis, it is worth thinking about knowledge from other topics which may be relevant. It is also important to try to respond to *all* aspects of the source material. So, in this case, consider the significance of there being one Green MP and the fact that there are 26 Bishops of the Church of England in the Lords. The main pitfall to avoid would be answering a question that has not been asked. For example, you are not being asked to comment on *why* Parliament is unrepresentative, merely to evaluate how representative it is or is not.

Student A

> The source shows that the Conservative and Labour parties are over-represented in the House of Commons. They have a higher proportion of the seats than the votes they won. The Conservatives won about 36% of the votes in the general election, but won nearly half the seats. Labour won 29% of the votes but about 40% of the seats. The Lib Dems won 22% of the votes but only about a fifth of the seats. So the Commons is not representative of the party strengths. The Lords is even worse as there are more Labour peers than Conservatives. However, there are more Liberal Democrats in the Lords so they are better represented. The coalition government represents a majority in the House of Commons, but this is not possible in the Lords. In the House of Lords there are 26 bishops, which shows that the Church of England is well represented, but this is false because the other main religions in the UK are not so well represented.
>
> In the Commons all 650 constituencies are represented by an MP but peers do not represent a constituency. MPs do represent their constituencies well on the whole and every individual can feel that their MPs will take up their cause. Many of the peers, however, have a special knowledge of one aspect of society or represent groups and pressure groups in society such as medicine, education, industry, finance, religion and the law. Many of these are crossbenchers and so are independent and able to represent groups instead of parties. MPs tend to toe the party line and so are less representative. In this sense we can say that the Lords, although it is not elected, is actually more representative than the Commons.

ⓔ **9/10 marks awarded:** 6/7 for AO1 and 3/3 for AO2. This A-grade answer achieves a good balance between the material in the source and the student's own knowledge. For example, use is made of the party strengths in Parliament, but the answer also refers to the votes cast for the parties at the last election (this question could only have been attempted by a student who had studied Unit 1). The student notes that many peers have no party allegiance, as shown in the data from the number of crossbenchers, but the student also knows, from their own knowledge, what kinds of groups are represented by these kinds of independent peers. The student also writes about constituency representation, which is not shown in the source. So, very good marks are gained for AO1 (not quite full because the candidate should have described a little more fully party representation in the Lords) and full marks for AO2. This is because there is both good analysis — why the two Houses can be described as representative or unrepresentative, and good evaluation — the extent to which each House is or is not representative. A good evaluative aspect is comparing the two Houses in this respect.

Student B

The House of Commons is not very representative at all. This is mainly because of the electoral system that favours the two main parties but discriminates against the Liberal Democrats. We can see that the Lib Dems have far too few seats and that Labour in particular has too many. In the House of Lords there is a much better balance with the Lib Dems having nearly 100 seats, which is closer to their true representation. We can also see that, at last, the Green Party has some representation, but not enough because of the unfair electoral system. In the Lords the crossbenchers hold the balance of power, which is representative because it prevents one party being able to dominate completely. This means that peers can be really representative because they cannot be so dominated by the government, as happens in the Commons. If we turn to the bishops we can possibly say that the Christian religion is over-represented. This is because it is the established religion in the UK but it does not reflect the religious make-up of the country any more. The House of Lords is not representative, of course, because it is not actually elected, unlike the Commons. Finally, we can see that Labour has the biggest group in the House of Lords and this is clearly unrepresentative because Labour actually lost the 2010 election.

ⓔ **5/10 marks awarded:** 3/7 for AO1 and 2/3 for AO2. The main problem with this answer is that not enough 'own knowledge' has been used. Note the contrast with the A-grade answer, where the candidate is aware of how and why the Commons is so politically unrepresentative. This answer also fails to examine and analyse whether the House of Lords is representative, even though it is not elected. The answer is reasonable at looking at the data shown, but does not go very much beyond it — more 'own knowledge' is required. There is some analysis and evaluation, but not strong enough for the top AO2 mark. The A-grade answer scores well on AO2 by comparing the two Houses and is a little more critical. This answer achieves a grade C.

(c) How could the representative role of Parliament be improved?　　　　　(25 marks)

ⓔ Take care over your introduction and end with a good conclusion. It is a mistake simply to launch into the content. In the body of your answer, it is good to use original ideas but this should not be at the expense of fundamental issues.

Student A

Before considering this question, it is necessary to consider what the term 'representative role' actually means in the context of Parliament. It can mean a number of different things. First, it means that Parliament is a true reflection of the party strengths in the country. Second, it refers to how well constituencies are being represented by their MPs. Third, it means that Parliament should perhaps be a microcosm of society as a whole. This is called social representation. Fourth, it can mean whether Parliament represents the national interest. Parliament obviously does some of these things well and others badly. This essay will consider how matters can be improved in each case. **a**

The main problem with the House of Commons is that party representation is distorted. In order to make it more representative of the parties we would have to change the electoral system. Ideally this would be to proportional representation so that the votes cast would be represented accurately by the number of MPs for each party. However, this is unlikely because it would lead to constantly hung parliaments which most people fear. **b** It could be that only the House of Lords will be elected by PR so that it is a representative body. Even if it is appointed, the membership of the Lords could be made to represent the party voting strengths more closely.

MPs have a good reputation for representing their constituencies on the whole, so little needs to be done. A proposal to allow constituents to recall unsatisfactory MPs could be used, as in parts of the USA. Otherwise perhaps, if the electoral system were changed, MPs might be made to be more accountable. **c** Perhaps Parliament could set aside more time for MPs to raise constituency business.

Making Parliament more socially representative is different. Some have argued for women quotas to ensure more are elected to the Commons, but this has always been opposed. It is easier to make an appointed second chamber more socially representative, so there is room for improvement there. The Appointments Commission could ensure that more members from ethnic minorities, younger people and people from diverse backgrounds could be chosen as well as more women. **d**

Finally, how to make Parliament represent the national interest more? The House of Lords can do this now as it is more independent of party control. MPs, on the other hand, tend to be slaves to the party line. The only way would be to weaken the control that party whips have over MPs which is not easy. If MPs had an alternative career path to simply becoming a minister, they would be more free of the power of patronage and so could think more independently. Perhaps also there should be more free votes when the whips are called off and MPs can follow the national interest. But party leaders are reluctant to do this.

So we can see that there are a number of measures that could be adopted. These include a change to the electoral system, controlling membership of the House of Lords, women quotas, the power to recall MPs who do not represent constituencies well and the use of more free votes in the Commons. The most important of these has to be a change in the voting system to make the Commons more politically representative. **e**

ℯ 20/25 marks awarded: 6/8 for AO1, 7/9 for AO2 and 7/8 for AO3. The main strength of this answer is its very clear structure. **a** It makes a good start, with the student deconstructing the question and defining the term 'representative'. The introduction is followed by logical content and **e** a sensible conclusion, summing up the content and picking out one key idea. **c d** The answer loses 2 marks on AO2 mainly because it does not fully develop the electoral reform argument (a good point is made but not explained) and is not able to explain more fully how to introduce more diverse candidates. It covers enough ground but could have been a little fuller with knowledge and understanding, perhaps by including more material on the representative role of the House of Lords, which was a little weak. **b** The comment about people's fear of hung parliaments is unnecessary — the question is not asking for evaluation. Overall, an A-grade answer.

Student B

The main way in which the representative role of Parliament could be improved would be to change the electoral system. **a** The first-past-the-post electoral system favours parties with concentrated support such as the Conservatives and Labour. It also means that small parties such as the Lib Dems, the Greens and the BNP or UKIP do not have chances to win many seats. This means that Parliament is unrepresentative because small groups and parties are under-represented. If we introduced proportional representation as we have for European elections, there would be many parties represented in Parliament. PR might also increase the number of women and MPs from ethnic minorities because, if a list system was used, there would be opportunities for the parties to include such people. PR could also be used for elections to the House of Lords in the future. This would help it to become less elderly and male dominated.

If STV was adopted as a system each constituency would have as many as six MPs. This would significantly increase representation by allowing citizens to choose which MP should represent them. As things stand, constituents have to accept the MP who has been elected. Voters do not have any say in which candidates should be adopted. If there were a primary system, as in the USA, voters would feel better represented. **b**

We could make the House of Lords more representative if we ensured that the appointments to the Lords took account of the different groups in society, such as different religions, women and ethnic minorities. The House of Lords could also then represent the national interest more effectively. It might be possible to have quotas for such different groups. We could also introduce quotas for women and ethnic minorities in the selection of party candidates for the House of Commons.

In conclusion, we can see that there are a number of measures which could be adopted to make Parliament more representative.

ⓔ 13/25 marks awarded: 4/8 for AO1, 6/9 for AO2 and 3/8 for AO3. This barely makes a grade C. It has strengths and weaknesses. **b** The strengths are that it has a number of interesting and unusual points and relates them well to the question, hence the relatively high AO2 mark. (There are plenty of marks for such originality, as long as it is accurate and relevant, as in this case.) It also explains the suggestions well and covers both houses of Parliament. **a** Its weaknesses are that the structure is poor, with no introduction (which is an important failing) and a weak conclusion. There is also no sense of development, hence the low AO3 mark. On AO1 its range is not wide enough. It does not tackle the really key issue of how MPs can carry out their representative role more effectively. It concentrates excessively on social rather than functional representation.

Question 4 **Essay-style question**

Assess the arguments in favour of an elected, or partly elected, House of Lords. (40 marks)

e Try to avoid the major and common pitfall of not answering the precise question being presented. It is vital to think about the exact wording of the question and to respond to it. Questions which ask for an assessment of an argument expect an answer that looks critically at those arguments rather than one undertaking a balanced evaluation.

Student A

Since the 1990s there have been many calls for an elected House of Lords. The main groups in favour of such a move have been the Liberal Democrat Party, many members of the Labour Party, the pressure groups Liberty and Unlock Democracy and a small number of members of the Conservative Party. Then in 2010 David Cameron came out in favour and the reform of the House of Lords was included in the coalition agreement. The main arguments in favour of an elected or partly elected chamber have been: to make it more democratic, to make it a better balance to the power of the government and because it could bring into politics more of the smaller groups and parties who cannot get into the House of Commons. This essay will examine these and other arguments and will assess their strengths and weaknesses. **a**

The first argument is that the current House of Lords which is a mixture of appointed life peers and hereditary peers plus some bishops is hopelessly undemocratic. In fact it has no legitimacy at all. The Lords is part of the legislative process and scrutinises legislation and government policy, but none of its members have been elected and none of them are accountable. Although the Lords cannot veto legislation or force through amendments, it has no democratic right to act on behalf of the people. **b** Holding elections for the Lords (which would probably have to change its name, perhaps to the Senate) would correct this problem. However there are problems with this. Most important is that the second chamber might simply be a mirror to the House of Commons. What is the point of having two elected chambers? One answer is to elect the second chamber by a different system to first past the post. This would mean that the second chamber would have a different political make-up to the Commons. It would almost certainly guarantee that the governing party would not have a majority and so Parliament would have a balance.

The second argument is that the second chamber would become a more effective balance to the power of government. **c** As I have said above the government would not have a majority in the second chamber and so could not simply steamroller legislation through with the whips forcing MPs to follow the party line. A more independent second chamber could look more critically at proposed legislation. government would have to ensure that there was a consensus of support for a measure. This is very much how things work in the USA where the President has to secure support for legislation from both houses of Congress which represent all elements of political opinion. This does have a major problem. It could be that government would simply find it too difficult to pass legislation and there would be a lengthy deadlock. **d** One of the advantages of the British system of executive dominance is that government can be decisive and efficient. For example it can easily pass its budgets and most foreign policy measures are supported. As we said in the USA this can be difficult and much reform has been prevented because of such deadlock (for example over health reform or gun control).

The third main argument is that it would bring in smaller groups and parties. This would depend on PR being used. PR would bring such parties as the Greens, UKIP and Nationalists. These parties are mostly excluded from the Commons (though the Greens won one seat in 2010). The second chamber would then better represent such views as environmentalism, nationalism and anti-European ideas. These views are under-represented as things stand. However, there is a major problem. PR might also bring into politics some extreme parties such as the BNP. This would give publicity to ideas which we might not find acceptable, though some would argue all political views should be heard, even if we don't like them. We have to ask, what would happen if an extremist Islamic Party gained some seats in the second chamber?

One additional, perhaps weaker argument, is that elections to the second chamber could act as a mid-term opinion poll for the people, demonstrating how they feel about the government's performance. This is a role of mid term elections in the USA. It is, however, a weak argument, because people nearly always tend to express opposition to governments in mid term, even though they still support them broadly. So there might be 'false' results in elections to the second chamber.

On the whole an elected or partly elected second chamber seems to be very attractive, but there are a number of serious drawbacks. For example it may be that people would grow tired of too many elections and turnout would be very low. We would also lose many of the very effective appointed peers that we have now, such as Lord Winston, who speaks about medicine or Lord Putnam who knows so much about the film and TV industries. These people would probably not stand for election and so would be lost to politics. **e**

In conclusion we can see that there are some very powerful arguments in favour of an elected second chamber. There is also a case for a partly elected chamber as this might act as a compromise between the present situation and a totally elected chamber. There are also some important problems with these proposals. However the strengths of an elected chamber seem to be overwhelming. In particular it is the need for an effective check on government, properly elected which tilts the argument in favour of reform. **f**

@ **40/40 marks awarded:** 20/20 for AO1, 12/12 for AO2 and 8/8 for AO3. Full marks for this near perfect A-grade answer. **a** It has a logical structure and an excellent introduction that sets the scene, sets out the ground and states how it will be approached. **c** It then follows the structure referred to in the introduction, covering as much of the ground as is reasonable in 40 minutes (there are other points to be made but not all could possibly be discussed in the time available), and **d** answers the question by critically assessing the arguments. **e** The question requires a concentration on the arguments in favour but, to assess them, some of the opposite arguments need to be mentioned briefly, as is done here. **b** The writing is very good with excellent use of political language and concepts — legitimacy, democracy·and accountability. Illustrations are used to good effect. **f** Finally, there is a strong and decisive conclusion.

Student B

The arguments concerning an elected or partly elected chamber are quite evenly balanced. There are three main arguments in favour of reform and three main arguments against. This essay will examine these arguments and decide finally which side of the argument should prevail. **a**

The first argument is to make the second chamber more democratic. At the moment the Lords is appointed, with some hereditary peers, and so cannot be called a democratic chamber. The peers do not really represent anyone and are not accountable for their actions. The Lords are often required to pass legislation and amendments to legislation, but they do not have a democratic right to do this.

The second reason for an elected second chamber is that it would act as a balance to the 'elective dictatorship' which operates in the House of Commons. The government can get its legislation through the Commons because it is able to control its own majority. Even with a coalition the government was in complete control. If the second chamber did not have a government majority, the government would have to 'win the argument' and persuade the members of the Lords to support them. This would improve the democratic legitimacy **b** of the whole process.

The third reason is that it would give an opportunity for the people to express their feelings about the performance of the government between general elections. By electing opposition members or people from small parties the electorate would be saying that they were dissatisfied (the same kind of thing happens in America every 2 years).

There are also strong arguments against. First, it might be possible that an election to the Lords would simply replicate the result in the Commons. This would cancel out the advantage of the second chamber acting as a check to executive power. This would not always happen and proportional representation could be used to prevent it, **c** but many say what is the real point?

Second, it would mean that many peers who now sit in the Lords and have special knowledge and experience would not stand for election and so we would lose their valuable input. These peers play a special role in proposing useful amendments and improving legislation.

Third, it may be that the electorate would not turn out in large numbers. People may not think that such elections are important and they may become tired of having to vote so often. If the Lords was elected on a low turnout it would not have democratic legitimacy. It is also true that people nearly always vote against the government in by-elections and local elections and they would do the same in elections to the Lords. This would mean the government would nearly always do badly. Of course this has an advantage in that it would be a check to the power of the executive, but it might also cause a great deadlock. **d**

In conclusion we can see that the argument about an elected second chamber is very evenly balanced. An assessment is therefore to say that yes many argue for an elected second chamber, but there are equally strong counter-arguments.

ⓔ **22/40 marks awarded:** 12/20 for AO1, 5/12 for AO2 and 5/8 for AO3. There is a reasonably large amount of relevant information here so the mark for knowledge and understanding (AO1) holds up quite well at 12 (it still lacks real world illustrations). However, this C-grade response has three major problems. **a** One is that it is producing a balanced discussion when the question requires concentration on the arguments in favour of an elected second chamber. This problem is immediately apparent in the introduction, where the student is not answering quite the same question but is doing a pros and cons of reform instead of assessing the arguments in favour. (Compare this with the approach of the A-grade answer). **c** A second problem is that it fails to develop and analyse properly the implications of using proportional representation, which is a pity as this is a key point (handled well in the A-grade answer). Thus the analysis is weakened. Third, the answer scores only 5/8 for communication because the structure breaks down and there is no logical journey towards a firm conclusion. **b** There is, however, some good use of political language. **d** A good point is made in the penultimate paragraph, but the essay is now losing its structure — this should have been discussed earlier.

The prime minister and cabinet

Question 5 Stimulus-based question

Study the following sources and answer the questions that follow.

Source 1

Cabinet government

The term 'cabinet government' was, for many years, used as a description of the centre of British government. It implied that the cabinet was the centre of decision making, that central government took decisions on a collective basis and that the cabinet is collectively responsible for all decisions made. The doctrine of collective responsibility further requires that all members of the cabinet defend decisions that they have made among themselves. In effect they must 'toe the party line' or face dismissal. It also implied that the prime minister was merely primus inter pares, that is a senior policy-making figure who, nevertheless, held the same status as other cabinet ministers.

Source 2

Prime ministerial government

This theory, which became popular in the 1960s, suggested that the prime minister was more than just the most senior member of cabinet. It meant that the prime minister is a separate policy maker who is also able to dominate his or her cabinet. It implies that the prime minister has his or her own sources of authority and has powers far beyond those of the cabinet. Furthermore it suggests that the prime minister is separately accountable for government policy.

(a) From the sources, outline any two differences between the terms 'cabinet government' and 'prime ministerial government'.

(5 marks)

ⓔ Generally it is wise to avoid merely quoting from the sources. It is much preferable to use your own words to express the facts and ideas contained in the sources. By all means use some of the wording from the passages, but try to add something of your own to make a further clarification.

Student A

The first difference is that with cabinet government it is the cabinet itself that is the central policy-making body. Therefore it is right at the centre of the political system. Prime ministerial government says that the prime minister himself is at the centre of policy. The second difference is that under cabinet government decisions are made collectively by all ministers and they are all collectively responsible for them, whereas with prime ministerial government decisions are often made by just one individual — the prime minister and he (or she) is individually responsible.

ⓔ **5/5 marks awarded:** all for AO1. Two very clear differences are identified and they are expressed in the student's own words, giving us a little more information than the mere words of the sources. Grade A.

Student B

1. Cabinet government implied that the cabinet was the centre of decision making. The prime minister is a separate policy maker.

2. 'The cabinet is collectively responsible for all decisions' whereas 'the prime minister is separately accountable for government policy'.

ⓔ **3/5 marks awarded:** all for AO1. The student has correctly identified two of the differences. However, these are simply quoted from the sources and are not explained in the student's own words. 3/5 is a good enough mark, making this a B-grade answer, but a little extra information would have gained all 5 marks.

(b) From the sources and your own knowledge, explain the operation and importance of collective responsibility.

(10 marks)

ⓔ Remember to include at least one example in your answer. It is also important to distinguish between material from the source and 'own knowledge'. This question calls for the difficult skill of analysis. A tip is to think of *why* something happens or is important. Another possibility is to think and explain the *consequences* of a practice or a principle. Both ideas will gain AO2 marks.

Student A

Source 1 clearly explains that collective responsibility means that the cabinet is collectively responsible for all its decisions. The source also states that this implies that ministers have to publicly support all the decisions that the cabinet has made collectively. It says that they must 'toe the party line', which means they have to agree with party policy and that, if they do not, they may be dismissed from the government. **a**

Ministers may disagree with proposals in private and argue about them in the privacy of the cabinet, but once the cabinet has made a final decision it becomes official policy and all ministers (not just cabinet ministers) must support those policies in the media and when talking to the public. Sometimes a minister wishes to disagree publicly in which case he or she must resign. This occurred when Robin Cook disagreed with the invasion of Iraq when he was foreign secretary. He resigned and became a backbench MP. **b** The reason for this is that they have agreed to be accountable for decisions collectively. All cabinet meetings are held in secret so it is safe for a minister to disagree in private but then support policy in public.

Under coalition government collective responsibility is more difficult and so Lib Dem ministers have been given permission to disagree over some policies such as the raising of tuition fees and nuclear energy policy. It would have been unacceptable for Lib Dems to support policies they had campaigned against in the previous election (though there were many problems over tuition fees). However the Lib Dem ministers still have to accept cabinet policies once they have become official.

ⓔ **10/10 marks awarded:** 7/7 for AO1 and 3/3 for AO2. Full marks for an excellent A-grade answer with several strengths. **a** First it makes a clear distinction between material from the source and 'own knowledge'; the first paragraph specifically identifies material as coming from the first source — this is a good practice. Own knowledge in this case is both development of the information in the source and entirely original points. Second, it is up to date, discussing the coalition. **b** Third, it uses an appropriate example, the Cook resignation — essential for a top-mark answer. Fourth, it uses analysis by explaining how and why collective responsibility is so important. Hence it receives all 3 AO2 marks.

Student B

Collective responsibility is the doctrine which says that all ministers are collectively responsible for all decisions made by the government. What this means is that they must agree in public and if they do not they may be dismissed by the prime minister. Sometimes ministers resign so that they can disagree in public. **a** Ministers often disagree in private but they must 'toe the party line' in public. When ministers stand up in Parliament or give an interview on TV or to a newspaper they are only allowed to repeat what is official government policy. Under the coalition there have been some exceptions to these rules and Lib Dem ministers have been allowed to disagree in public, though most of them have fallen into line. Collective decision making means that ministers discuss policy and come to a consensus decision which they are all prepared to support in public. It also means that they all stand or fall together.

ⓔ **5/10 marks awarded:** 4/7 for AO1 and 1/3 for AO2. This answer has some merits. In particular it is a clear and accurate explanation of what collective responsibility means. So, it receives 4/7 for AO1. However, it does not distinguish between material from the source and 'own knowledge'. The student should have picked out the relevant information from the source as the A-grade student clearly does. **a** It does not use an example, although it is up to date on coalition government. The answer gains only 1 mark for AO2 because it virtually fails to analyse why collective responsibility operates or to analyse its effects. Overall, this is a C-grade response.

(c) How important is the modern cabinet? (25 marks)

ⓔ Even if you wish to come to a very specific and one-sided conclusion you do need to give both sides of an argument a good deal of space. Having presented a balanced argument, by all means reach a firm conclusion on one side or the other, but make sure you explain why you have reached that conclusion, for example by identifying the 'clinching' argument.

Student A

The cabinet traditionally stands at the centre of British government. It is part of the core executive. It is made up of over 20 senior ministers who are appointed by the prime minister. Whenever they reach a decision about policy, that policy becomes official government policy. Cabinet is appointed and chaired by the prime minister. However, many have argued that the cabinet is no longer the important body it once was. This essay will consider and compare the arguments that suggest it remains important against those who claim it is less significant. **a**

It is still true that all important decisions have to be 'cleared' through the cabinet and that they are not legitimate unless the cabinet approves them. It may be that proposals have been made by the prime minister or by cabinet committees etc. but they are not official policy until the cabinet has approved them. It is also true that, in times of emergency, the cabinet meets to deal with the situation. This often occurs in times when there is armed action by British forces, as in Iraq or Libya. It is also true that the doctrine of collective cabinet responsibility makes government strong because it makes it united.

On the other hand, there is much evidence that cabinet has become less important. Its meetings have become less frequent and they are shorter. But the main reason for this belief is that the centre of policy making has moved outside the cabinet towards the prime minister and the many private advisers who now operate in Whitehall. The prime minister, it is claimed, can control the cabinet because he (or she) appoints its members and can dismiss them. The PM also controls the agenda and therefore has great influence over its decisions. Ministers are not often willing to defy the prime minister. Tony Blair was well known for his 'sofa politics' whereby he would discuss policy with a few chosen colleagues outside cabinet and then present the cabinet with a 'fait accompli'.

So we can see that there are arguments on both sides. The cabinet is certainly not as important as it used to be but this is not to say that it has no importance at all.

ⓔ **17/25 marks awarded:** 5/8 for AO1, 6/9 for AO2 and 6/8 for AO3. This answer achieves a grade A, though with not much to spare. It is logically set out and has a reasonable range of arguments on both sides of the evaluation. However, there are a number of issues that could, and should, have been raised. These include the many functions the cabinet has in addition to policy and decision making, the renewed importance of the cabinet under coalition and the fact that prime ministers do not always dominate the cabinet, as was the case with John Major and Gordon Brown. The analysis is reasonable, though it perhaps should have been stated that the influence of cabinet will ebb and flow and the reasons for that could have been analysed. AO3 marks are good, with plenty of appropriate political language used. **a** It begins with a good enough, clear introduction, setting out the ground, but possibly both the introduction and the conclusion could have been fuller.

Student B

It is true that the cabinet used to be the central decision-making body in the UK. However, this has now been largely replaced by prime ministerial government. The prime minister is now something like a president and so the cabinet is correspondingly less important. This essay will explain how this process has occurred. **a**

Under the premierships of Tony Blair and Margaret Thatcher, in particular, the prime minister was very dominant. **b** Many decisions were made by the prime minister himself, often using sofa politics, private advisers and 'kitchen cabinets'. Under Tony Blair the cabinet met just once a week and only for about 45 minutes. Indeed it was often said that the cabinet had just become a 'rubber stamp' for decisions made by the prime minister. Under coalition government the same is true, with decisions being stitched up between Clegg and Cameron.

It would be wrong to say that the cabinet does not do anything. It does occasionally deal with emergency situations, but this is only when the prime minister allows this to happen. In most case the prime minister does not resort to a cabinet decision, but instead prefers to make his own decisions. In addition he has prerogative powers which mean he does not have to consult cabinet at all.

In conclusion we can see that the cabinet is no longer a very important institution. It has largely been replaced by prime ministerial government. Only when government is deadlocked in some way does the cabinet become an important institution. **c**

e **13/25 marks awarded:** 4/8 for AO1, 5/9 for AO2 and 4/8 for AO3. **a** This answer has one overwhelming fault, evident right from the outset — it is unbalanced. There is no problem in coming to one particular conclusion, either that cabinet is insignificant or that it remains important, but the other point of view must be presented. **b** For example, John Major and Gordon Brown could have been mentioned in paragraph 2. The answer has some strengths as a presentation of one side — that the prime minister dominates — but it otherwise pays too little attention to the possibilities that the cabinet remains important. **c** The last comment almost rescues the evaluation — it shows some sensitivity to a counter argument — but it is not enough. Overall, this response achieves a C grade.

Question 6 Essay-style question

To what extent is it reasonable to describe modern British prime ministers as 'presidents in all but name'?

(40 marks)

ⓔ Think carefully about the wording of the question and respond to it precisely. It is also extremely important to use conceptual analysis. Here that means such ideas as accountability, authority, political leadership and presidentialism. Refer back to the question in your conclusion.

Student A

We must first ask what is meant by the term 'president'. **a** A president is a head of state. This means that he or she can speak on behalf of the whole nation. A president also has his own source of authority and is answerable directly to the people. In fact presidents are normally separately elected. In contrast a prime minister is just a head of government and can only speak on behalf of the government. This essay will consider whether the modern British prime minister is effectively a president even though he will never be the head of state. It will also consider the many ways in which this view may be mistaken and that there is an 'appearance' of presidentialism, but that there is no substance to this view. **b**

Prime ministers certainly enjoy prerogative powers — the arbitrary powers of the monarch which she no longer exercises but delegates to the prime minister instead. These include the power of patronage (ministers, peerages etc.), the power to be commander-in-chief, to wage war and to negotiate with foreign powers and organisations such as the EU. When the prime minister is exercising these prerogative powers, he (or she) does indeed look like a president. He can act without consulting his cabinet or Parliament. This happened when Cameron intervened in Libya by sending the air force. He also negotiated with the other powers over the no-fly zone.

Many prime ministers also adopt a presidential 'style'. Blair and Thatcher were typical. They were very keen to deal in foreign relations and so were using the prerogative powers to the maximum. Thatcher led Britain into the Falklands war while Blair brought us into Kosovo, Iraq and Afghanistan. Both these prime ministers, as well as Cameron, have had a very high profile abroad, just as presidents do (like Obama and Sarkozy).

There has been a massive growth in the amount of advice available to prime ministers. The Downing Street machine, containing many advisers and committees, looks very much like the White House set-up. This means the prime minister has sources of independent advice, just as presidents do. The cabinet has become insignificant and at times it seems that prime ministers are governing alone. Even under coalition this still seems true.

Finally, it is also true that the public and media today treat the prime minister as the main spokesperson of the government. Michael Foley has called this 'spatial leadership', where the prime minister is separated from the rest of the government, rather as a president is.

There are, however, arguments against this presidential view. Above all the prime minister is not head of state and cannot speak on behalf of the nation. We saw this when Cameron led the campaign against the huge government budget deficit in 2010. He claimed to speak for the nation, but many said he was simply operating Conservative party policy and many people opposed the plans. In other words, he was head of government but not of state. **c**

Above all, though, we have to say that not all prime ministers are so dominant. Gordon Brown, for example, certainly looked presidential when leading the response to the global financial crisis in 2008, but in the UK he became weaker and weaker and less and less presidential. John Major was also a weak prime minister, largely because he had enemies in his own cabinet and he lost his parliamentary majority. Major and Brown certainly also did not have a 'presidential style'. **d** It also has to be said that a prime minister has limitations which a president does not. He can be overruled by his cabinet or by his close party colleagues. In extreme circumstances (as with Thatcher) he may be removed from office by them while a president has a fixed term and is only answerable to the people. In a peculiar way, too, the prime minister is actually *more* powerful than a president in that he generally controls the majority in parliament while a US president may well be overruled by Congress, as has happened a few times with Obama. Prime ministers do not have a separate source of authority from the rest of government. They are also constantly accountable to Parliament while a president is not. **e**

In conclusion, it is clear that there are a number of angles to this question. In conceptual terms, the prime minister is certainly not a president. In practice some prime ministers have behaved in much the same way as a president. It is also true that, for reasons explained above, prime ministers have become more dominant. On the other hand, we have also seen some non-presidential prime ministers and there are powerful restraints on prime ministerial power that a president does not face. But it can be said that the prime minister is not a president, not in name and not in substance. Some PMs may have given the appearance of a president but they remain heads of government. The main reason for reaching this conclusion is the fact that a prime minister is constantly accountable to Parliament, to cabinet and to his party. A president has considerably more freedom of action and so can dominate more effectively.

ⓔ 37/40 marks awarded: 18/20 for AO1, 11/12 for AO2 and 8/8 for AO3. An excellent A-grade response, nearly full marks. Its strengths are a first-class introduction, a logical structure with **d** good balance and a first-class conclusion. **a** It makes a good start, **b** explaining and deconstructing the question and setting out the proposed answer. **c** It uses plenty of up-to-date illustrations and **e** makes excellent use of conceptual knowledge and analysis. The posts of prime minister and president are both well analysed. A couple of AO2 marks are lost because there could have been a little more detail on the premierships of Brown and Blair and there could also have been a little more analysis of Blair's experience. Full marks for AO3 because it is excellently written and constructed and there is a great deal of use made of appropriate political vocabulary.

There is no doubt that the prime minister has become a more dominant figure in British politics since the 1960s when the term 'prime ministerial government' was first used. **a** Many say that this has happened so much that the prime minister can now be described as a president. This view will be examined in this essay.

There are many ways in which prime ministers have become more dominant:

First, they have begun to dominate cabinet more and more. Cabinet meetings are getting shorter and less frequent and many of the decisions are decided by 'sofa politics' and the use of many special advisers. Prime ministers control the agenda and have great powers of patronage to appoint and sack ministers. This means they are very loyal to him and he can control what they do.

The public and the media also look at the prime minister as the embodiment of the government. This means being a spokesperson and that it is the prime minister who is the main policy maker. We know that political leadership has become increasingly important, as illustrated by the leadership debates before the 2010 election.

There have also been a number of very dominant prime ministers in recent years. Tony Blair and Margaret Thatcher were important examples. They used foreign policy matters to be dominant and both fought important wars in the Falklands and Iraq and Sierra Leone. These adventures also made them seem much more presidential. **b** Blair and Thatcher were also ruthless in packing the government with their own supporters.

There are some counter-arguments to this. Not all prime ministers are so dominant. John Major had a small majority in Parliament and Gordon Brown became unpopular and there were many plots against both of them. It is also true that prime ministers can sometimes be overruled by Parliament or by the cabinet. In extreme circumstances a prime minister can be removed, as happened to Thatcher in 1990. There is also the 'elastic theory' of power which states that, the more power a prime minister claims, the more powerful become the forces against him. This happened to both Blair and Thatcher in the end. **c**

There is also an issue of 'style' — some prime ministers have a presidential style of governing alone and in a dominating way, while others do not. Brown certainly did not have this style and seemed constantly uncomfortable being prime minister. Once the public and the media lose confidence in a leader, as happened to Brown, they certainly do not look presidential.

In conclusion we can certainly say that prime ministers do often look presidential, but not enough to be able to say they are presidents in all but name. Some individuals may be close to this, but on the whole they are not. **d**

e **22/40 marks awarded:** 12/20 for AO1, 5/12 for AO2 and 5/8 for AO3. The main problem here is that the student is answering a rather different question. The answer is discussing how dominant prime ministers have become. **a** This is apparent from the beginning, where the comment is true but an alarm bell rings — the question is about presidentialism, not prime ministerial government (similar but distinct concepts). **b** This impression is slightly saved with a belated reference to the actual question — there was a danger the answer was drifting away. The answer also fails to analyse the issues conceptually. The analysis is, in other words, rather shallow. **c** There is some balance, and plenty of use made of examples but, again, not in a well-developed way. **d** The conclusion is weak. Above all this response falls down on both AO1 and AO2 because too much of the material is not focused on the question. None the less, the conclusion should have referred back to the question and given a relevant assessment. This is a C-grade response.

Judges and civil liberties

Question 7 **Stimulus-based question**

Study the following source and answer the questions that follow.

The Supreme Court

The Supreme Court came into being in the UK in 2009 as part of a package of reforms contained in the 2005 Constitutional Reform Act. The Supreme Court differs from the former judicial functions of the House of Lords in a number of ways. First there is no automatic right for its judges (12 in number) to sit in the House of Lords. Indeed, it is an intention of the Act to separate the senior judges in Britain's highest appeal court from the legislative process. Second, new appointments to the court will be made by a special committee of senior legal figures and so will be removed from any possibility of political interference. Third, the court has its own president who is not a politician. In the past the Lord Chancellor, a cabinet minister, was head of the judiciary, but this is no longer the case. As the most senior court in the country, the Supreme Court has a number of roles including the interpretation and protection of civil liberties, the upholding of the principles of the rule of law and ensuring that the government and other public bodies do not exceed their legal powers.

(a) From the source, outline two ways in which the independence of the judiciary has been improved.

(5 marks)

ⓔ It is easy to get beyond 2 marks for questions like this. The first 2 marks, which ask you to identify two pieces of information (occasionally three), are simple and there are no hidden pitfalls. All you need for the other 3 marks is a little explanation in your own words.

Student A

First, the source says that the new Supreme Court has been separated from the House of Lords where the highest appeal court used to be. This means that judges are no longer in two branches of government — the judiciary and the legislature. Second, there is a committee which will appoint new judges. The source suggests that politicians will not be on this committee so there will be no political interference.

ⓔ **5/5 marks awarded:** all for AO1. A very clear, simple and accurate A-grade answer, mostly expressed in the student's own words.

Student B

The new Supreme Court is one measure and the other is that the Lord Chancellor is no longer the head of the legal system.

(e) **2/5 marks awarded:** both for AOI. This is a D-grade answer, scoring only 2 marks. These are awarded for accurately identifying two measures, but no extra marks are given because there is no explanation.

(b) From the source and your own knowledge, explain the importance of the Supreme Court. (10 marks)

(e) Remember to read the question carefully and respond directly to it. Here the question refers to 'importance'. It is therefore important to *focus* on importance rather than producing a merely descriptive answer. Always attempt some analysis: the question usually directs you to what kind of analysis is required.

Student A

The source identifies a number of key roles for the Supreme Court. First it is the highest court in the legal system. All other courts must follow its rulings. This system is known as judicial precedence. The source says that the court interprets laws. This is a crucial role. Interpretation of the law, in effect, develops new law. The most senior judges in the Supreme Court can use all their experience in interpreting the meaning of laws. The importance of this is that all other courts must follow the same interpretation. This would apply, for example, in cases where the European Convention on Human Rights is being interpreted. When the court does this it also upholds the rule of law. This means ensuring that everyone is treated equally under the law and this is a key part of any modern democracy. In cases of judicial review the court also upholds civil liberties and controls the power of government. So it hears appeals from citizens that their civil liberties have been abused by the state or the newspapers or any other body. They may also claim that the state or a public body has exceeded its legal powers. These are *ultra vires* cases. Because the Supreme Court is the highest court its judgements in these cases is binding on all other courts.

(e) **7/10 marks awarded:** 5/7 for AOI and 2/3 for AO2. This just about deserves a grade A. It outlines the kinds of cases heard by the Supreme Court and there is an analytical understanding of judicial precedence and how it works. It identifies the correct material from the source, but does not expand enough from the student's own knowledge. For example, the constitutional role of the court should have been explained, as should its role as an independent check on government power. The operation of the Human Rights Act should have been briefly explained and perhaps a real case or two should have been quoted.

Student B

The role of the Supreme Court to be found in the source includes the following: it interprets and upholds civil liberties, it imposes the rule of law, making sure that all are treated equally under the law, and it prevents the government and other state bodies from exceeding their legal powers so it is a check on the power of government.

From my own knowledge I can say that the Supreme Court is important because it makes judgements on the Human Rights Act. If individual citizens feel their rights have been abused they can appeal to the Supreme Court and hopefully have their rights respected. The Supreme Court hears all cases that have great importance. In addition the court will hear *ultra vires* cases. This is where it is claimed that a state body has acted beyond its legal powers. The court is important because it can reverse such a decision. The state bodies have to obey its decisions.

ⓔ **5/10 marks awarded:** 3/7 for AO1 and 2/3 for AO2. This response merits a grade C. It correctly identifies the key roles of the Supreme Court, but it does not develop or illustrate these roles sufficiently. There are also no real-world examples. In particular, its main weakness is that it does not explain *why* these roles are important (the A-grade answer does this, albeit briefly). It merely states what the important roles are but does not express clearly enough the central and authoritative role of the Supreme Court.

(c) Explain the operation and importance of judicial review.   (25 marks)

ⓔ Where there is a concept in the question (in this case judicial review), it is always good practice to define that concept. Once again, it is worth emphasising the importance of using real-world examples. This is a general revision tip — try to learn some examples to illustrate all the main topics.

Student A

The term judicial review is extremely important in legal terms. **a** It refers to a process where a citizen or a group of citizens appeals to the courts on the grounds that they have been the victims of a miscarriage of justice of some kind. The main examples of such problems are that civil liberties have been abused, that a state organisation or the government has acted beyond its legal powers (*ultra vires*), that citizens have not been treated equally or that proper procedures have not been followed when making a decision which affects citizens.

So, the first reason that judicial review is important is that it provides a means by which citizens can seek redress. **b** What is more, the judgements made by the courts in such cases will become law and will be enforced in all other similar cases. So, in the Belmarsh case, once it was declared illegal to hold terrorist suspects for long periods without trial, the ruling of the court became binding on all police forces in the UK in all circumstances. **c** Judicial review also upholds the rule of law. Citizens can ask for a review on the grounds that they have not received equal treatment. This has been the case with cancer victims claiming they had been denied drugs when other patients had been prescribed them (Herceptin). **d** All state bodies therefore know they must be careful to treat people equally.

It is vital that the state and government operate within their legal powers, otherwise there is a possibility that government could become uncontrolled. The threat of judicial review ensures that public bodies do not exceed their powers. Reviews also ensure that proper procedures are followed (for example when considering planning applications), or a citizen will launch an expensive review.

In conclusion, judicial review is important because it gives the courts the ability to protect citizens' rights and to control the excessive power of government.

ⓔ **22/25 marks awarded:** 6/8 for AO1, 8/9 for AO2 and 8/8 for AO3. This is an excellent A-grade answer that focuses directly on the central issue — why judicial review is important. **a b** It refers to this right at the beginning and again later in the response, and again in the conclusion. **c d** There are excellent examples of judicial reviews used to good effect and the consequences of such reviews are explained well. The only significant omission is a fuller explanation of how the Human Rights Act works and therefore the reviews connected with that. The response is very well written and so there are full marks for AO3.

Student B

The courts are the means by which the rights of citizens can be protected and government can be prevented from exceeding its powers. There have been big increases in the use of judicial review in recent years and these have increased the role of the judiciary. We can now look at what kind of judicial reviews have been used. **a**

The most important example is the upholding of rights. If an action or decision by government may have abused the European Convention on Human Rights citizens may go to court and the court may declare that the action should not be allowed and possibly should be reversed. However, the courts cannot overturn a parliamentary statute. Citizens can also claim that they have been treated unfairly and this should be reviewed. If the courts uphold the appeal it means that the citizen can enjoy redress.

Everybody must be treated equally by the state and a citizen can appeal to the courts if this is abused. Again the courts can order that a decision be changed. This is very important for citizens to feel they are protected from government which is treating them unfairly.

So the importance of judicial review is that it can protect the rights of citizens and prevent the government from abusing its powers. Citizens can also use their MPs, but then there is no guarantee of redress. However, if a court makes a ruling, the state must always do something about that ruling

ⓔ **15/25 marks awarded:** 4/8 for AO1, 6/9 for AO2 and 5/8 for AO3. This is a good answer, worthy of a B grade. It has two faults, however. **a** One is that, in spite of a promising start, it fails to define judicial review. The second is that it is not comprehensive enough — it does not give examples and it does not examine all the circumstances where judicial review may be used. So there are only 4/8 marks for AO1. It loses some AO2 marks because it does not analyse quite fully enough the importance of judicial review, though it does do some accurate analysis. Only 5 marks are awarded for AO3 because the structure is not logical enough, especially the opening.

Question 8 Essay-style question

To what extent can, and should, judges control the power of government? (40 marks)

ⓔ With questions like this, the answer should have two clear parts. The first part ('to what extent can…') is descriptive and so carries more AO1 marks, while the second part ('to what extent should…') asks for evaluation, which scores more highly on AO2. Take such factors into account in your answers.

This question has two parts. The first asks how it is that judges can control government power. This is done in a number of ways and these will be explained in this essay. The second question asks whether judges are the right people to do this. The alternative to judges controlling government is mainly Parliament, so this essay will ask which is preferable. **a**

Judges (the courts) can control government in a number of ways. The first is by imposing the Human Rights Act. All actions by government must conform to the European Convention on Human Rights and if a citizen believes that his or her rights have been abused he or she can ask for a judicial review and may have the decision overturned. This obviously prevents the government from simply ignoring rights. If it were not for the courts and judges, the government would not necessarily respect these rights. **b**

There are also *ultra vires* cases where the judges can rule whether the government has exceeded its powers. An example of this occurred in 2009 when the Supreme Court judges ruled that the government did not have the legal power to freeze the assets of suspected terrorists because they were not convicted criminals. The famous Belmarsh case was similar a few years before. **c**

Judges can also decide on cases of miscarriages of justice which may have been committed by the state. This means that the rule of law is maintained. In all the above cases the judges are using judicial review to control government power.

The main alternative to judges controlling government is Parliament. MPs often take up the grievances of citizens and can also debate and vote on proposals, which may help to control state power. The difference between Parliament and judges is that MPs are elected and accountable, whereas judges are not. Furthermore the judges are not very representative of the whole population. They are all elderly or middle aged, middle class, male and white. At least MPs in Parliament tend to be more varied. More importantly MPs are in constant touch with their constituents and so can be sensitive to public opinion. In contrast judges may be out of touch and so do not understand public opinion.

On the other hand, judges are independent and, on the whole, neutral. This means they are able to apply the law without bias. MPs have their own political aims and so may act in their own interests. Worse still, MPs on the government side are whipped and tend to toe the party line. They are therefore not in a good position to control government power.

Finally we can turn to the question of whether judges have actually become too powerful. **d** It can be argued that it is up to government how we treat offenders and suspected terrorists because they have the responsibility for maintaining order in the state. Often, too, the rights of citizens may be excessively protected so that government cannot do its work effectively. **e** Some say government is constantly being obstructed by these unelected and unaccountable judges.

In conclusion this essay has shown how judges can control government power and has considered the question of whether judges are the right people to do so. On balance it seems important to maintain the power of judges. They are neutral and are in a good position to uphold rights and justice, independent of political interference.

ⓔ **27/40 marks awarded:** 12/20 for AO1, 8/12 for AO2 and 7/8 for AO3. This answer just makes a grade A. It is well structured and written and so scores well on AO3. **a** It makes a great start — dissecting the question, recognising the two parts and explaining how the answer will proceed. **d** It also does quite well on AO2 because it does analyse the role of judges reasonably well and evaluates the role of judges as against politicians. However, the analysis should have gone further, particularly looking at how limited the role of Parliament inevitably is and, conversely, how the power of the judges has grown. The weakest area is on AO1. **b c e** This is partly because there are not enough examples (there are two good examples in paragraph 3, but none in paragraph 2 nor in the penultimate paragraph where an interesting point about excessive protection of rights does need one). The answer also falls down at AO1 because it does not deal comprehensively enough with the various forms of judicial review.

Student B

There are a number of ways in which judges can control the power of government. These include the following: **a**

First they can use judicial review. This is where a citizen claims that justice has been abused by government. If the judges rule in favour of the citizen this acts as a control on government power. It may be that the government has acted against the European Convention on Human Rights. Thus the judges can ensure that government takes the Human Rights Act into account. Second, there are *ultra vires* cases. This is a direct way of controlling government power. If it is believed that government has acted above its legal powers the judges can review the actions and can strike them down. Also the judges may abuse the constitutional principle of the rule of law. The judges can rule that a citizen has been treated unequally.

Now we can turn to the question of whether judges should control the power of government. The main issue here concerns law and order and anti-terrorist actions. If the judges are constantly preventing the government taking action by insisting on human rights then the community is put at peril. Why should a judge have the power to decide on political issues such as anti-terrorist actions? It should be the elected government that decides when rights need to be protected and when the whole community needs protection.

On the issue of stopping the government exceeding its powers, it would seem that Parliament is better placed to deal with such issues. Government is meant to be accountable to Parliament, not to judges. The powers of government should be in the hands of Parliament which grants such powers. **b** Furthermore, if we had a codified constitution, that would effectively control government power without the need for constant intervention by judges. **c**

In conclusion, judges are there to make sure that justice is maintained together with human rights and the rule of law. They have strong powers to uphold these principles. There is, however, an argument that suggests that these powers are excessive and that the balance has shifted too much towards the judges. **d**

e **17/40 marks awarded:** 8/20 for AO1, 5/12 for AO2 and 4/8 for AO3. This is a rather weak D-grade answer with a number of faults. **a** It starts badly with no introduction. Although it does address both parts of the question, it lacks any depth in the explanations, which are all very thin. **b** Though some good points are made (if not well expressed), there are virtually no real-world illustrations. On the second, more analytical part of the question, it misses the key issue of whether unelected judges should have so much power. **c** There is an analytical discussion, but it contains dubious, vague assertions and does not deal with fundamental questions about the judiciary. The writing quality is relatively weak and little political vocabulary is used.

On the plus side, after the first paragraph, there is some sort of logical structure. **d** The conclusion, though a little thin, is not bad and does reflect what is in the body of the answer.

Knowledge check answers

This section gives you summaries of the answers to the knowledge checks contained in each topic. You can see how accurately and comprehensively you were able to answer the questions.

1 You should have found three of these:
- To establish the distribution of power between various institutions
- To establish the rights of the citizens
- To establish the limits to the power of government
- To explain the relationships between political institutions
- To set out rules for how the constitution can be amended
- To establish the nature of the state and how an individual can be or become a citizen

2 Parliamentary sovereignty is important for these reasons:
- It places Parliament at the centre of the system.
- It establishes what is the source of all political power — Parliament.
- It means that constitutional principles cannot be entrenched because Parliament cannot bind its successors and is not bound by its predecessors.
- Parliament is the ultimate source of all law even though it delegates law making to subordinate bodies such as local government and devolved assemblies.

3 Legal sovereignty still lies with the UK Parliament at Westminster. However, in reality, sovereignty has become dispersed:
- Parliament has surrendered some legal sovereignty to the EU. It can take it back only by leaving the EU.
- Because government usually controls its own majority in Parliament, it becomes *effectively* (though not legally) sovereign over key decisions.
- At the time of elections or referendums it can be said that sovereignty reverts to the people.
- Though no *legal* sovereignty has been devolved, *political* sovereignty has been delegated to the Scottish Parliament and the Welsh and Northern Ireland assemblies.

4 In one sense the UK has not lost sovereignty because the UK can leave the EU and so restore all its own sovereignty. However, the UK has lost sovereignty over some areas of jurisdiction, such as agricultural subsidies, fishing rights, trade, employment, law and consumer protection. In areas not transferred to the EU, the UK retains sovereignty. In practice, EU law is binding on the UK and must be enforced by the British courts.

5 Your three choices should be included in the following criticisms of the UK Constitution:
- The constitution is uncodified and therefore unclear, too flexible and does not adequately control government power and protect civil liberties.
- It grants too much power to the executive branch.
- There is a lack of the separation of powers.
- The electoral system produces unrepresentative government and Parliament.

6 The areas of constitutional reform which Labour failed to complete after 1997 were as follows:
- Electoral reform, promised in the 1997 manifesto, was not implemented at all.
- House of Lords reform was limited to removing most hereditary peers.
- Devolution granted some powers to devolved government, but not law-making powers to Wales and Scotland.
- The Human Rights Act was not made binding on Parliament.

7 The main distinctions in function between the Commons and the Lords are as follows:
- The Commons can veto legislation; the Lords can only delay it for 1 year.
- Commons amendments are binding, but Lords amendments need Commons approval.
- There are departmental select committees in the Commons but not in the Lords.
- The Lords has more time for long general debates on great issues.

8 Select committees have the role of scrutinising the work of government and government departments. They do so on a non-partisan basis. Legislative committees are partisan and consider proposed amendments to legislation.

9 Government controls the House of Commons in a number of ways:
- The government controls most of, but not all, the business of the House.
- The government is normally able to whip its own majority into line and so is unlikely to lose a vote.
- Party loyalty means that the government can normally rely on support for its proposals.
- The government whips generally control voting in the legislative committees.
- The government is able to block any attempts at unwanted private members' legislation.

10 The House of Lords is relatively weak for these reasons:
- It can only delay, not veto, legislation.
- It has no jurisdiction over financial issues.
- Its proposed amendments can be overturned in the House of Commons.
- It lacks democratic legitimacy.
- The government can manipulate membership to its own advantage.

11 Reform of the House of Commons has become important because there is so much public disillusionment with politics. Reform of the Commons may go some way to restoring public confidence in politics and MPs.

12 Reform of the Lords is controversial mainly because politicians cannot find a consensus on what to replace the current chamber with. Liberals want a radical change while Conservatives are more cautious. The House of Lords itself also tends to obstruct reform.

13 Collective responsibility is important for a number of reasons:
- It gives government a strong sense of unity.
- It enables the prime minister to control the cabinet.
- It prevents major splits in government.
- It enables the government to speak with one voice.
- It controls dissidents at the centre of government.

14 Prerogative powers are important because they form the basis of much of the prime minister's authority. They enable the prime minister to act decisively, especially in times of crisis or emergency. They also give the prime minister wide powers of patronage and so underpin his or her power generally.

15 Individual ministerial responsibility is important because it ensures that someone in government can be made responsible for what occurs. It avoids situations where no one is held accountable for problems and errors. It also acts as a discipline on the conduct of ministers.

16 A head of government is leader in terms of government policy. He or she can speak only for the government and not the whole nation. He or she can be removed by Parliament. The head of state can represent the whole nation and is directly responsible to the people. The head of state represents the nation irrespective of politics, while a head of government is a specifically political figure.

17 Recent prime ministers have become more presidential in a number of ways:
- They are increasingly seen as spokesperson for the whole government.
- They play an increasingly leading role in relation to the media.
- Some recent prime ministers have adopted a presidential style.
- They increasingly dominate the political system.
- They often claim a separate source of authority to the rest of government (spatial leadership).
- They now have access to a large range of independent advice in the Downing Street 'machine', much as the US president does.
- There is increasing emphasis on foreign affairs, making the prime minister appear more presidential.

18 Judges 'make law' in these ways:
- They interpret existing law and so can change and clarify its meaning.
- They apply law to specific cases and so create what is known as 'case law'.
- They establish the nature and meaning of unwritten common law.

19 The European Court of Human Rights interprets and enforces the European Convention on Human Rights (ECHR), which was established by the Council of Europe. The European Court of Justice interprets and enforces the laws of the EU.

20 Judicial review is important because it offers citizens access to the courts so that they can establish their rights, appeal against injustices or unequal treatment, or can claim that a public body is exceeding its powers. It is therefore vital in the preservation of civil liberties, the rule of law and legal limits to the power of government.

21 The Supreme Court is important because it can be seen to be independent from government and Parliament. It is the highest court of appeal in the UK and its decisions are binding on all lower-level courts. It is a vital part in the interpretation and protection of constitutional principles, the rights of citizens, the limits to government law and the rule of law.

22 Judicial neutrality is important because, if judges are truly neutral, they will dispense justice without favour to any individuals or groups in society. It is also essential if cases of political importance are to be resolved fairly and without political bias.

23 The Human Rights Act is important for these reasons:
- It establishes a codified and clear set of rights for citizens.
- It guides the courts in judgements which involve human rights.
- It helps prevent governments abusing civil liberties.
- It is binding on all except the UK Parliament.

24 The fact that judges are neither elected nor accountable is important because judges often make judgements which have wide social and political implications. As they are not elected, judges cannot be made accountable for such vital decisions. It can be argued that it is the elected Parliament that should ultimately rule on key issues such as human rights, the dispensing of justice, how to deal with criminals and terrorists, and what are the appropriate limits to the power of government.

Index